C000023671

The Forking Trolley

An Ethical Journey to
The Good Place

JAMES M. RUSSELL has a philosophy degree from the University of Cambridge, a post-graduate qualification in critical theory, and has taught at the Open University in the UK. He currently works as director of a media-related business. He is the author of *A Brief Guide to Philosophical Classics* and *A Brief Guide to Spiritual Classics*. He lives in north London with his wife, daughter and two cats.

The Forking Trolley

An Ethical Journey to
The Good Place

James M. Russell

PALAZZO

This edition first published in the UK in 2019 by
PALAZZO EDITIONS LTD
15 Church Road
London SW14 9HE
www.palazzoeditions.com

Text © 2019 James M. Russell
Design and layout © 2019 Palazzo Editions Ltd
Illustrations by Diane Law

All rights reserved. No part of this publication may be reproduced in any form or by any means – electronic, mechanical, photocopying, recording or otherwise – without prior permission from the publisher.

This is an independent publication and is not associated with or authorized, licensed, sponsored, or endorsed by any person, entity, or product affiliated with *The Good Place*. All trademarks are the property of their respective owners, are used for editorial purposes only, and the publisher makes no claim of ownership and shall acquire no right, title, or interest in such trademarks by virtue of this publication.

Book ISBN: 9781786750792
eBook ISBN: 9781786750877
Printed and bound in the UK by CPI

Contents

Welcome!
Everything is fine.

Introduction

This book is inspired by the brilliant TV comedy *The Good Place*, which combines surreal humor and a twisting storyline with a sincere attempt to consider the question "what does it mean to be a good person?" In the first episode we meet **Eleanor Shellstrop** (Kristen Bell) in the moments after her undignified death (she was stooping to pick up her bottle of Lonely Gal Margarita Mix for One in a parking lot when a line of shopping trolleys shunted her in front of a truck carrying a mobile billboard for Engorgulate, an erectile dysfunction treatment). She meets the eternal being **Michael** (Ted Danson) who assures her that, while most religions only got what happens after death "a little bit right", she definitely is in "the Good Place" rather than "the Bad Place".

As we see in various flashbacks, Eleanor has actually lived a pretty mediocre life, treating her friends and acquaintances with disdain, and rarely acting out of anything other than self-interest. We later discover that her original plan for the night she died had been to sit on her own at her house watching wedding fails videos on the Internet and drinking her cocktails through a straw "until I pass out on top of my vibrator".

Realizing that a huge mistake has been made (albeit a fortunate one for her) she asks her supposed soulmate **Chidi Anagonye** (William Jackson Harper) to teach her how to be a good person so that she can avoid being discovered and sent to the Bad Place. As a professor of ethics and moral philosophy he is particularly well placed to help her, but also paralyzed by uncertainty (and anxiety-induced stomach aches) when it comes to deciding what the right path of action is.

Of course, this is only the starting point of a long complex journey, but the key point is that throughout the first two seasons the show never loses sight of the question of what it means to be good (and this seems set to continue, given the fascinating set-up for the next phase of the show).

This book is intentionally written to avoid relying on or giving away the entire plot so that it might be understood by someone who hasn't seen the show. However, it should be noted that it is more or less impossible to write about the many staggering narrative twists and turns in *The Good Place* without risking some degree of spoilers (by, for instance, mentioning other "Places" or revealing the identity of particular characters), so please don't expect a perfect veil of ignorance¹ to be in place.

So, while the show will be referenced, it will be as a brief introduction to moral dilemmas and questions that can also be approached from other angles. From a broader viewpoint, we are going to take a journey through some of the main strands of ethical thought, with reference to 21ˢᵗ century moral dilemmas in particular.

Fun Facts: **The Main Characters**

We'll introduce more characters as we go, especially those who appear later in the show's run, but besides Eleanor, Michael and Chidi the most prominent initial characters are:

Tahani Al-Jamil (Jameela Jamil) a beautiful English socialite and charity fundraiser whose kindness and desire to do good are sometimes undermined by her rampant namedropping: she can boast that Princess Diana is one of her many godmothers, Beyoncé is her best friend, and she

---

1 Spoiler! The "veil of ignorance" is a term used by the philosopher John Rawls, who imagines an idealized way of creating a just society: citizens co-operate to come up with a set of moral rules to be derived from an "original position" in which they don't know what gender, talents, race, interests, wealth, or status they will have in that society (this is an example of social contract theory – see p.17).

has even travelled on James Franco's ironic trolley (which shuttles between his penguin grotto and the "garage of adult tricycles") while her name apparently means "Welcome Beautiful".

Jianyu Li/Jason Mendoza (Manny Jacinto), who we first meet as a Taiwanese Buddhist monk who has sworn a strict vow of silence and thus seems like a slightly odd soulmate for the loquacious and superficial Tahani. As the season progresses we will come to see him in a very different light . . .

Janet (D'Arcy Carden), the charming resident "informational delivery system", a kind of robot Siri, who looks and sounds like a very smiley human and can be summoned at any moment from her void to help the residents of the Good Place with (almost) any problem they might encounter.

Everything is Fine!

An Overview of Moral Philosophy

Imagine you are gliding high above the field of ethical thought (and have succeeded in dodging the flying shrimps and the exploding turkeys along the way...) Beneath your wings, you might see something that looks a bit like the map overleaf which shows the terrain.

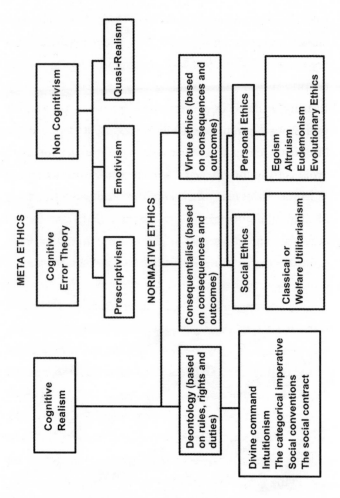

A crazy-high[2] birds-eye view of ethics

---

2 In the episode *What's My Motivation?*, Eleanor is complimented on the "crazy-high points total" she has accumulated on Earth and responds by mentioning her nickname at high school was "crazy-high Eleanor".

OK, there are an awful lot of 'isms' in there, so before we launch into considering some of the **practical ethics** that are thrown up by *The Good Place* and by life in the 21st century in general, let's take a quick tour of the basics. Bearing in mind that everyone hates moral philosophy professors, I promise we will keep this brief . . . but a brief overview at this stage will make it easier for us to avoid getting too bogged down in those 'isms' later on.

Meta-ethics (the top layer of the diagram) is the study of the fundamental properties of ethical statements, attitudes, and judgments – the question of what kind of thing ethics even is. In other words, when I make an ethical statement, what am I actually saying?

There are various possible meta-ethical positions. A **non-cognitivist** theory is one that claims that when we make an ethical statement, it is really an expression of something else: for instance, a **prescriptivist** would regard the statement "Lying is wrong" as being equivalent to saying "You must not lie"; **emotivism** is the idea that we are actually just saying "Hurrah for honesty and boo to lying". And a **quasi-realist** would argue that when we say "Lying is bad" we are merely projecting our personal emotional attitude towards liars as though it is a real thing in the world.

By contrast, **cognitivism** is the idea that when we make an ethical statement like "Lying is wrong" we really are saying something meaningful, which can be either true or false. **Cognitivist error theory** starts from this point but then dismisses all ethical statements as being false. Both non-cognitivism and cognitivist error theory are dead ends in the diagram as they don't naturally lead on to questions of how to be good. However, **cognitivist realism** takes the truth or falsity of ethical statements seriously and does lead to questions like "how can I be a moral person?" and "what does it mean to be good?"

This takes us to the second layer, which would contain a large proportion of moral philosophers ancient and modern. This is **normative ethics,** the branch of philosophy that attempts to define how one should act and what it is to be good . . . While this isn't indicated in the diagram, cognitive realists can broadly be divided into **moral realists** (who believe a moral statement is objectively true or false) and **ethical subjectivists** or **moral relativists** (who generally think morality is a real thing but is judged subjectively by individuals or society). This suggests that saying "Lying is wrong" is closer to saying "I do not like liars".

Subjectivism can seem woolly, but there have been attempts to make it more rigorous, for instance by suggesting that the moral course of action can be defined with reference to the **ideal observer** – in other words the right thing to do is what a neutral person watching you would believe you should do.

However, at this stage, a more useful way to classify

the ethical theories in the diagram is by the basic method you use to judge whether something is good or not – for instance, should our ethics be based on our actions, our intentions, our character or the outcomes of our actions?

The question here is what defines moral virtue. There are three main starting points for this. A **deontological** view is one that looks for definite moral rules that we should always stick to, whether they be based in principles, duties or rights. One example would be if you believe in **divine command** – in a god or deity that has set the rules for humans in stone. Another would be Kant's **categorical imperative** in which the idea that you should only do to someone else something you would want them to do to you is treated as a natural, unarguable starting point for all ethics. The idea that morality is grounded in either the **social contract** or **social conventions** (where society collectively sets the moral rules) gives us another way of interpreting rights and duties based on how people actually live their lives, while **intuitionists** believe we can directly perceive good when we see it, in a kind of "A-ha!" moment of recognition.

The second branch of this layer is **consequentialism**. This means that rather than looking to the absolute rules of deontology, we need to consider the practical outcomes of particular actions – so what is good depends on the context, and this is how we should decide what to do. **Eudemonism** was an early example of this kind of theory – it suggested that happiness or well-being is the main goal of virtue, but we should judge a person by how well their actions maximize happiness. Versions of this idea are mentioned by the great Greek philosophers – for instance, the thinker Epicurus is mainly remembered for his claim that happiness is the ultimate goal in life. And Socrates, Plato and Aristotle taught you should pursue virtue, partly because they also taught that it would lead to happiness (or a good life).

From the 18th century onwards, **utilitarian** thinkers such as Jeremy Bentham and John Stuart Mill revisited this way of looking at virtue. **Classical utilitarianism** basically suggested that you could develop a kind of calculus by which you measured how much happiness and pain a given action would cause, and that the most moral action was the one that scored most positively. **Welfare utilitarianism** is a more economically specific branch which tends to identify happiness with economic well-being.

Utilitarianism is based on how actions contribute to society – for a more individualistic way of thinking about outcomes you can look to various types of **ethical egoism** (which suggests our primary aim should be our own happiness, but still allows for ways to condemn actions that clearly hurt others), **altruism** (which inverts this way of thinking, placing the needs of others above individual needs) and **evolutionary ethics** (which looks at ethics primarily as a biologically driven way of thinking).

The final branch of the second layer is **virtue ethics** – rather than being based on rules or outcomes, this defines morality through character or personality – the suggestion is that we should work on being honest, caring, kind, brave and so on, and then we will tend to make moral choices without requiring rules. This was the main way that the ancient Greeks (Socrates, Plato and Aristotle in particular) defined virtue, and their approach was widely adopted for many centuries before being revisited by recent philosophers who felt that systems based on rules or outcomes have too many loopholes. Virtue ethics also focuses on the idea that it is possible to practice being a good person – Chidi quotes Aristotle, for instance, comparing virtue to playing the flute, something you get better at when you practice it. So, in Aristotle's view, character is voluntary, and you are responsible for improving yourself.

So, that's the whistle-stop tour, and we will return to look at many of these ideas in various guises through the book. However, the next obvious question to ask is what kind of ethical theory is at work in *The Good Place.*

Fun Fact: **Doug Forcett Won the Closest Guess**

In their first meeting Michael explains to Eleanor that, when it comes to ideas about ethics and the afterlife, each of Buddhism, Judaism, Islam, Christianity, Hinduism, and every other religion guessed "about 5%" of the truth. Humanity's biggest exception turns out to be a stoner from Calgary, a kid called Doug Forcett. One night, when he was tripping on mushrooms, a friend asked Doug what he thought about the afterlife and he started ranting on about what he expected: during the course of this spiel, he astonished Michael and his colleagues by getting "about 92% correct". Michael is proud to have a portrait of him on his wall, with the subtitle "The Closest Guess".

The Ethical Framework of the Good Place

It's tricky to pin down exactly where the Good Place's ethics actually come from (and probably intentionally so, as the show aims to discuss many different aspects of moral philosophy). In the first episode, Michael explains to the newcomers how and why they have qualified for the Good Place, something that is reserved only to the most exceptionally virtuous people. He explains that throughout your life, every time you have made a decision about whether to cut someone up by driving in the breakdown lane, eat a sandwich, read a trashy magazine, or whatever, you have been watched and accrued a points total. Bad acts give you a negative score, good acts give you positive points.

On first sight this seems like a deontological set-up – it is clearly rules-based as particular actions have particular scores. You could also see it as being akin to karma, in which good acts gradually accumulate, leading (in several Asian religions) to the person winning release from the cycle of life and death.

On the other hand, Michael also says that the system is about "how much good you put into the universe" which feels closer to a consequentialist viewpoint, in which the key thing is the outcome of your actions. And this is reinforced by a freezeframe inspection of the list of good and bad things and their points totals on the screen as he gives his talk. If fixing a broken tricycle for a kid who loves tricycles is morally better than fixing one for a child who is indifferent to them, then it seems that outcomes must be part of the calculation as well as intentions. This would take it closer to a utilitarian viewpoint, in which we can (theoretically) calculate the exact positive and negative effects of an act we are considering, and choose accordingly.

But let's not forget this is a comedy drama: the list of

items also includes some notably arbitrary things which we can either take to mean 1) the writers are having a bit of fun with us here or 2) they want us to question how consistent the ethics of the Good Place really are, and consequently whether something may be askew. On an emotional level you may be able to see why being loyal to the Cleveland Browns gets you positive points, while supporting the New York Yankees is a no-no, but it doesn't make much moral sense. And while it's easy to see why stealing wiring from a decommissioned military base, ruining an opera by behaving boorishly, or "telling a woman she should smile more"[3] are "bad" it seems less obvious (but funny) to include overstating your personal connection to a tragedy that isn't connected to you, or using "Facebook" as a verb. And no matter how you feel about French people, how can stealing bread be worth -17 points while stealing a baguette is -20, simply because it's French? (The demons of the Bad Place have a real downer on the French . . .)

The same applies to the list of "good things" – hugging a sad friend or remembering your sister's birthday are clearly kind and decent, while planting a baobab tree in Madagascar is a worthy act (even if it is only available

---

3 Note that the demonic Trevor, who arrives from the Bad Place in episode 8, *Most Improved Player*, is quick to tell Eleanor she should smile more, a neat reference back to the list of good and bad things.

to a lucky few). But other items seem to be based on idiosyncratic personal bugbears, such as the reward for maintaining your composure in a queue at the Houston water park, or for ignoring a text message while talking to an actual person.

The picture gets murkier when Eleanor complains to Chidi about not being able to swear properly (the Good Place will only allow her to say words and phrases like "motherforking", or "son of a bench"). He replies that cursing is prohibited in the neighborhood because a lot of people don't like it (to which she replies "That's bullshirt.") This sounds a lot like contractarianism (see p. 94), in which, to paraphrase, people within society have a veto on rules they don't like. This is a version of the social contract, which takes us back to an approach based on rules rather than outcomes, since it is about how we establish a moral code that everyone accepts.

Chidi himself mostly takes a Kantian view on morality – Immanuel Kant argued that morality is based on the categorical imperative. This is essentially an update of Jesus's golden rule ("Do unto others as you would want them to do unto you.") Kant uses a complex philosophical framework to claim that this rule gives us an objective, definite underpinning to all morality and that we need to start from there and derive all moral rules from it. On this basis Kant defines certain actions (such as lying) as being simply wrong (because we couldn't possibly want to live in a world where we could never trust others not to lie to us).

Of course, this kind of rigidity creates a lot of moral quandaries. In season 2, when Chidi must briefly pretend to be a demon in the Bad Place, he is initially paralyzed by his reluctance to tell a lie, no matter how good the outcome of that lie might be. (He eventually finds a way to soothe his own doubts and go along with the pretense by advising his "fellow demons" that the best way to torture their chosen victim is to make them constantly read philosophy books, which he describes as "thinking outside the bun", in a reference to the Taco Bell advertising slogan).

Another complication is that Eleanor's journey in the show is about simply becoming a better person rather than learning a set of rules or basing all moral judgments on outcomes. One tiny moment of moral progress comes when she is excited to realize she has waved the person behind her in the frozen yogurt line through so she doesn't hold up the line, rather than taking as long as she could to spite anyone who might complain about her (as she would have done in her mediocre past). Any further progress she does make is often based on the most basic of moral decisions – try to see the other person's point of view, try to do the right thing, and act for the right reasons instead of in the hope of getting something in return.

If the world of *The Good Place* wasn't so explicitly

based on a set of rules and points, this might lead us to conclude that the real aim here is for Eleanor to learn "virtue". At the very least we can suggest that when she attempts to learn from Chidi how to "be good", she is following feebly in the footsteps of the ancient Greeks, who saw personal virtue as being the path to happiness and a better life in general.

So, in the end, there is a bit of everything at work in the ethical universe of *The Good Place* – and that is probably for the best. The purpose of the show isn't to give us a prescriptive idea of morality, but to talk us through dilemmas and problems and to encourage us to think for ourselves about those issues. Chidi's lectures, and the books referenced by the show may provide us with a few hints as to the writers' own opinions, but on the whole, this is a show that asks questions more than it provides answers.

Is This a Simulated World?

Some viewers have noted that the closest comparison in our world to the points system used in the good place comes in video games. Games such as BioShock and Mass Effect award points for actions – for instance a player may be given negative points for killing an innocent character in pursuit of an in-game reward. This creates a philosophically flawed, but reasonably effective way of creating an internal ethics for a simulated universe. This observation (together with moments in episodes such as *The Trolley Problem* where Michael instantly conjures up an alternative simulation) has led some viewers to question whether the world of *The Good Place* is supposed to be a simulation. On the other hand, it's not difficult to find scientists, geeks and even entrepreneurs such as Elon Musk (whose underwater mansion Tahani has, of course, visited) who have advanced the idea that our *real* world may be no more than a Matrix-style simulation, so maybe it's best to just see how the story develops . . .

Rock, Paper, Scissors

We've already seen how complex the field of ethics is and how many different approaches to the subject there are to choose from. One of the reasons that "people hate moral philosophy professors" is that the subject of ethics rarely provides us with definite answers – more often it just raises insoluble problems. Chidi is the stereotypical academic philosopher – he has strong moral principles, but they often leave him in a state of hopeless indecision in practice. On page 1000 of his unfinished, unreadable book about philosophy he starts an entirely new section with the words "Of course the exact opposite might be true . . ." As a child he could waste an entire recess failing to choose a single player for his soccer team. He spent

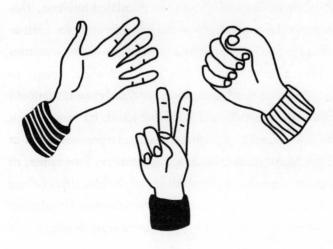

hours dithering over ordering in a restaurant (citing the "ethical ramifications" of different types of soup). He never chose a name for his dog – when it ran away he had to put up posters saying, "responds to long pauses", he can't even make a choice in a game of rock-paper-scissors, instead having a panic attack because there are so many variables to think about.

At one stage Michael uses the old psychologist's trick of imposing an arbitrary solution so that the subject can recognize if that choice feels right or not. Rather than tossing a coin, he makes a random choice from one of three flavors of frozen yogurt to jolt Chidi into making a choice. (The flavors are standing in for the "tres girls", each of whom has declared their love for Chidi in the episode *Chidi's Choice*).

Even then, Chidi fails to decide, the only result being that when he later comes across the trio (spoiler alert), Tahani, Real Eleanor and Fake Eleanor, all he can mumble is "Hey, it's my … three favorite yogurts."

Is this level of complexity and indecision what we want from ethics teachers? When they teach us about ethics, the starting point is often to outline a wide range of different meta-ethical positions and different ways of understanding moral codes, but they will never tell us which position they think we should choose. They never commit to saying, "this is what to do, and these are the reasons why," like a priest or parent might do.

Practical ethics requires us to make decisions – like, should you steal your neighbor's diary, throw a petrol bomb at your enemy's yacht, or kill the local informational system robot? But the advice from ethics is often complicated and unclear when it comes to practical action and even more so when it comes to dealing with even thornier issues like war, animal rights and capital punishment.

So, what is ethics for? Some philosophers have claimed that if you understand that something is morally right it would be simply irrational not to do it. Yet we can see for ourselves that people can be both irrational and deliberately "bad".

It's probably better to think of ethics as a moral map, and a way to think more roundly about disagreements. If we can be clear about what we agree and disagree on, it is easier to debate an issue rationally and calmly.

Ethics won't give us a simple "right" answer, and often it will give us several different ways of answering the same question. But we can use the framework of ethical theory to understand what exactly we are arguing about and this may be a start towards clarifying our positions or possibly even changing them. (Though bear in mind you can study ethics for a lifetime and still fail to persuade other people to agree with you. At one point Michael describes a situation in the show as being as rare as a double rainbow, or someone on the Internet admitting that they were wrong).

So, bear in mind that while the academic side of ethics can be befuddling, the goal in the end is simply to learn how to make good decisions, and how to practically and sensibly learn to be a better person. And if we can at least start there, we might gradually be able to move on towards the more idealized goal . . . of becoming the *best* person we can possibly be.

Fun Fact: **The Bad Place**

If Chidi, Eleanor, Tahani and Jianyu made it to the Good Place, who went to the Bad Place? It turns out that an awful lot of people did. At various times Michael informs us that its residents include

Mozart, Picasso, Elvis and pretty much every artist who ever lived, all the American presidents other than Lincoln, and even Florence Nightingale, although that one was marginal. Janet also pops up with one of her occasional fun facts, pointing out that Christopher Columbus wasn't such a close call and is in the Bad Place because of "all the raping, slave trade and genocide".

Choose Your Fro-Yo!

We've seen that a lot of people come to ethics hoping to be told "how to be a better person" and end up disappointed that that isn't how it works. Moral philosophy professors like Chidi give us a menu of moral choices, but we always end up having to choose our own frozen yogurt.

So, it's worth taking a few moments to look at why the objections and complications raised by ethics professors can genuinely help us to have a clearer understanding of what "being good" even means, and why so much of ethics seems to consist of philosophers pointing out the flaws in each other's arguments.

Let's go back to that basic question of whether morality should be based on rules, outcomes or character. The fundamental reason why these different approaches exist is that, whichever we initially choose, it is possible to find an objection to that approach – once again, this is

a bit like a game of rock-paper-scissors, in which each of the three approaches can seem to win in some scenarios but will fail in others.

The oldest way of defining morality was in terms of character. Aristotle believed that you could learn to be a better person, because your actions are under your own control. (Incidentally, Aristotle should be pronounced to rhyme with "bottle", not "chipotle", as Eleanor discovers early in series 3).

The problem with this definition is that it can seem somewhat circular – a good action is essentially defined as "something a good person would do". But different people, cultures and societies have different ideas of what is virtuous in the first place, so how are we to judge whether our current morals and virtues or those of our culture are "right" or "wrong"? If people sincerely believed that it was morally acceptable to own a slave in the past, how can we say we don't believe that was a "good" thing to do.

We might respond to this lack of clarity by deciding that a rules-based system is the best way to define our morality. Whether we follow divine command, the categorical imperative or the social contract, we end up with simple, unambiguous rules like "lying is always wrong" or "never break a promise".

However, we can immediately come up with situations that challenge these rules. If a doctor knows that a patient will only recover if they avoid stress, might he be better off telling a white lie reassuring them that they are definitely going to recover (especially if it is a lie which might help in that recovery)? If you could save ten people's lives by lying or breaking a promise, should you do so? Our basic moral intuition is that simple rules sometimes fail us.

For instance, Chidi knows he should never lie, but on several occasions finds that "social niceties" or "harmless lies" will do less harm than telling the truth, for instance after he mortally offends his sick friend Henry by finally telling him he hates his red boots: as Chidi's friend points out in a flashback, sometimes we lie just to be nice to people and stay friends with them.

Chidi also promises Eleanor he will always protect her, but this immediately involves him in all kinds of other moral quandaries, such as whether he should put loyalty to other residents of the neighborhood above his personal friendship. Even when he is trying to teach Eleanor the simple kindergarten rule of "don't steal stuff" and follows up by wondering whether he also might have to teach her not to throw sand, she responds with the excellent observation that throwing sand is a great way to put out a vodka fire.

It is even possible to come up with challenges to "Thou Shalt Not Kill" by envisaging a scenario in which it is clear to everyone that the killing is justified by circumstances. For instance, it can clearly be right to use force in self-defense or to protect others, but how do we judge the point at which this becomes immoral?

You can try to adapt rules-based systems by adding provisos: "don't lie, unless there is an overpowering reason to do so", for instance. But then how do you define the exceptions without leaving similar loopholes and getting into an infinite regress of counterexamples and unsatisfactory patches?

It is this kind of challenge to rule-based systems that led to the development of utilitarianism from the 18th century onwards. The idea was to quantify our instincts that tell us that it is sensible and ethical to judge situations on the actual effects of our actions rather than purely following a rigid set of rules.

Utilitarianism is an initially appealing idea – many

students who are introduced to it for the first time react like Eleanor in episode 5 (*Category 55 Emergency Doomsday Crisis*): "I like this one, it's simple!" The trouble is that, as Chidi responds, it's easy to imagine problematic counterexamples in which doing something highly immoral leads to a "good" outcome. Chidi points out that utilitarianism can justify taking one innocent life to save a hundred, or launching pre-emptive war. So long as you can argue that the good outweighs the bad, utilitarianism will bail you out of all kinds of evil deeds.

So, using either rules or outcomes to define morals leads to complications. And it is these shortcomings in other attempts to precisely delineate moral rules or methods that has led to a revival of interest in virtue ethics in recent years (see p. 89). But this simply takes us back to the start of the circle that led on to the theories we have already discussed.

So, there may be no perfect way to close the circle. However, by looking at what is wrong with each possible answer to the question "what is good?" we can at least come to a clearer understanding of how we think about morality and, more importantly, why we think it.

In the end your fro-yo may end up being a blend of a thousand different flavors, each of which has something to contribute to the final question of how to live a good life.

Chidi's Challenges

Moral philosophy professors are fond of giving their students a few questions or quandaries to go away and ponder at the end of their lessons. So let's end every chapter with a few of the questions that Chidi might ask his students.

1. Who do you think would win in a bar fight between a deontologist, a consequentialist and a virtue ethicist?

2. Have you ever used "Facebook" as a verb, taken off your shoes and socks on a commercial flight, or told a woman to smile more? Would you again?

3. How many points do you think you are up (or down) for your day so far – you can start off by giving yourself plus fifteen for reading this far . . .

Somewhere Else
Calculating the Consequences

It makes a lot of intuitive sense to consider the consequences of your actions as an important part of their ethical value. As Eleanor spotted, utilitarianism has the appeal of great simplicity. Add up all the happiness and pain that your actions will cause and act so as to maximize the balance. The trouble is that it is too easy to play the game of utilitarianism bingo to come up with a counterexample.

Utilitarianism Bingo

Imagine a judge who knows a defendant in a murder trial is not guilty, but also knows that an innocent verdict will result in riots that will cost one other person's life. Classical utilitarianism doesn't help us much here, as the net effect is neutral, so probably the judge should return the innocent verdict. But what if it will cost ten lives in the riots? What if it will cost a hundred lives? What if it will cost a hundred lives, but the judge's moral example will save two hundred lives in the future? Each time our judgment of what is "right" must be readjusted. Each adjustment must assume the judge has perfect knowledge of the future. And any time the calculus suggests the judge should condemn an innocent man to death it jars horribly with our sense of what "justice" should be.

Similarly, when Eleanor causes a trash storm through her selfish laziness, does the fact that some residents love clearing up trash make it OK? At one point in *The Good Place,* Eleanor refers to herself as a utilitarian nightmare because Chidi's duty to help her means every bit of her happiness at being spared the Bad Place leads to a huge amount of pain for Chidi, who may never find his true soulmate as a result. (However, as viewers, we also have to wonder whether this is fundamentally flawed – because what if Eleanor really is his soulmate and just doesn't know it yet?)

In the end there is a simpler way to think about the problem with utilitarianism. When Eleanor suggests that the ends might justify the means, Chidi points out this isn't a quote from someone worthy like Oprah, but from the amoral writer Machiavelli. Any time you find yourself agreeing with Machiavelli on ethics, you have to wonder whether something has gone badly wrong.

Jason and the Utilitarian Dilemma

One of the rare moments when Jason shines in Chidi's lessons on how to be a good person comes in the utilitarianism class. He points out he used to know a girl called Sheila who traded alligators on the black market and was going to marry "my boy, donkey Doug" and move to Sarasota. As Doug was a key member of Jason's street dance crew, he framed Sheila for stealing boogie boards and got her taken away to save the 60 people in his crew. Chidi is shocked to realize this is indeed a good example of the utilitarian dilemma, when doing one bad thing has good consequences for many other people so could be justified by the theory.

The Doctrine of Double Effect

As we saw in the previous section, it's all very well trying to analyze an action based on perfect knowledge of the future, but we are often in the same boat as the judge (who doesn't know what will happen after the innocent verdict) or Eleanor (who can't truly know if his assistance for her will cause Chidi future harm).

The **doctrine of double effect** is one way of trying to create a rule of thumb that can help us in practical situations. It states that if we do something that has a morally bad side-effect, it's not necessarily wrong, providing the bad side-effect wasn't intended (even if it was foreseeable as a possible outcome). The first known instance of the double effect argument came when Thomas Aquinas tried to come up with a set of rules for dealing with a case where a person might break the "Thou Shalt Not Kill" commandment in self-defense.

Today it is often cited in legally complex situations. For instance, while euthanasia is illegal in the UK, it can (in particular circumstances) be legal for a doctor to apply high doses of a painkiller that in fact lead to the patient's death. Doctors who disapprove of abortion may nonetheless feel it is OK to remove the fallopian tubes or uterus of a pregnant woman if the primary intention is to save her life, even though this will also kill the fetus. And, controversially, double effect has been used to justify civilian deaths in bombing missions, where the primary target was a military one.

The doctrine requires a few additional criteria – it can only be applied if the main act is either morally good or, at least, not morally wrong, the bad effects must not be disproportionately large, and the bad side effect must be unintended (even if it could have been predicted).

This final condition is very hard to define. When Michael is looking for a moral justification for killing Derek to avoid hurting Jason and Tahani, Chidi points out to him that killing is generally "frowned upon", and explains the doctrine of double effect. When Michael seizes on this as giving him a potential way out, Chidi points out that Michael's only intention should be the good outcome (saving the neighborhood), and that he can't simply "wink" while fully intending the bad outcome (the murder of Derek).

And this idea of "winking" pretty much nails the moral ambiguity of double effect. At what point does a doctor who "accidentally" kills a patient, while knowing full well what the fatal dose of a painkiller is, kill them on purpose? The debate on euthanasia seems stuck in a cycle of "winking" about the doctor's real intention when it might be more honest to accept that sometimes death by painkiller is the kindest outcome, even if it is fully intended.

Instead, in recent years, many UK hospitals chose the far more horrific "death pathway" in which nutrition was withdrawn, while different hospitals took very different views on the thresholds for letting patients die, with controversial results.

The case of civilian bombing deaths leads to some even more horrific cases of "winking". When we see government or army spokespeople justifying civilian deaths on the basis that "the terrorists were using the civilians as a human shield" we must ask whether the certain knowledge of the likely death toll should have been enough to rule out this action. As civilian deaths in bombing raids become more and more normalized, perhaps this is a case where double effect has been taken too far, and these spokespeople, like Eleanor when she wants to kill Janet, are convincing themselves they are doing "one small murdery thing" for a more important, significant reason.

Nonetheless, courts have to make decisions and there are many cases in which double effect, if clearly and carefully applied, can be the "least worst" way to deal with a problem where an action with a good outcome is also likely to have a bad outcome – the US Supreme Court has explicitly accepted double effect arguments in its rulings on medically aided death and it is likely to continue to be cited in cases far beyond Michael's botched attempts to get rid of Derek.

Fake News

In the 21st century, we are living in a Kantian nightmare. His suggestion that we could not will a world where no-one tells the truth is neatly demonstrated by the way that we are regularly bombarded with made-up news stories on social media, while the actual truth is often casually rejected by people who declare it to be "fake news".

What's the moral? Possibly that we shouldn't make the mistake of electing liars to high office? Or that if you spend your life treating the truth as being insignificant and making up the facts you want people to believe, no-one will know when to believe you in the future?

This is also a dilemma that Michael faces in the second season of *The Good Place* – when he casually suggests changing sides and helping Eleanor and her friends, the immediate question that needs to be asked is why they should trust someone who has been lying since the minute they met him.

Definite "No-Nos"

Ethics textbooks raise real or imaginary moral problems which are genuinely complex. And we can admit that some of the moral quandaries Eleanor faces are at least a bit tricky. Chidi may have qualms about killing Janet, but part of Eleanor's motivation is good (saving Michael). However, some of the flashbacks to her earlier life present us with moral challenges which should really be no-brainers – for instance, when she is looking after a friend's sick dog while she visits her sick mother, Eleanor is offered tickets to a Rihanna concert in Vegas: she can only go to the concert by leaving the dog a huge supply of food and it ends up so fat it is "bulbous" as a result. She also once abandoned her colleagues on a night out when she was supposed to be the designated driver (because she had hit it off with the barman), mocked her boyfriend for boycotting the local coffee shop (where the owner had been filmed sexually harassing women), and set her mailbox on fire so that the attractive mailman would have to take off his shirt.

On another occasion we watch in flashback as she purloins her housemate Madison's recently dry-cleaned dress and rips it while trying it on, before denying all knowledge and telling her that it's just the risk you incur when you try to keep your clothes clean: Madison sues the dry-cleaner for $900 plus an additional $80 million for emotional distress and puts them out of business in the process. When Madison then goes viral as "Dress Bitch", Eleanor and her other housemate make a hefty profit from printing and selling Dress Bitch T-shirts . . .

It doesn't really matter that Madison is a pretty awful person (you can tell because she has vanity license plates, one of Michael's "no-nos", and says "Ciao, bitches"); and it doesn't matter whether you follow Aristotle, Bentham, Kant, or any other philosopher – I think we can all agree these are pretty mediocre actions, and that Michael may have had a point when he closed Eleanor's file after hearing about the Dress Bitch incident and called for a one-way train to take her to the Bad Place.

On the other side of the coin, when Eleanor first meets her fellow residents of the Good Place and encounters a woman who apparently devoted her life to clearing landmines from the area surrounding orphanages when the United Nations wouldn't clear them, and a man who donated **both** his kidneys to someone he had just met on the bus, I think we can agree that these are unequivocally "good things". And if Eleanor really had been a lawyer who managed to get pardons for innocent people on death row, that would also have been decent behavior.

But the task of ethics isn't to identify some actions as obviously good or bad, but to nail down some of the reasoning we use when we make those judgments, to give us a clearer framework when it comes to the trickier moral decisions in life.

Fun Facts

When the almighty judge Shawn reviews Eleanor's record, the screen reveals a few more of her lifetime lows, including screaming at waiters, showing *The Shining* to a nine-year old (presumably traumatizing them in the process), being banned for life from the build-a-bear workshop, being a recidivist when it comes to heckling Santas in shopping malls, sneezing onto salad bars, giving away the endings of movies, subjecting a pregnant woman she met at spin class to cyberbullying, and, possibly worst of all her crimes, flirting on social media with Kid Rock.

Everything is Complicated

Going back briefly to utilitarianism, one of its major proponents, John Stuart Mill, was fiercely against the doctrine of double effect, although partly for cynical reasons. He argued we should never confuse the judgment of a good action with the judgment of the intentions behind that action: "He who saves a fellow creature from drowning does what is morally right, whether his motive be duty, or the hope of being paid for his trouble; he who betrays the friend that trusts him, is guilty of a crime, even if his object be to serve another friend to whom he is under greater obligations." Mill argued that if we closely consider our motives, there will almost always be some questionable side to them, whether it be the Christian who does good out of fear of hell, or the philanthropist who gives to charity partly to be remembered after they die.

Given that Tahani is depicted as being flawed for having raised £60 billion for charity (but partly for selfish reasons) and Chidi's focus on the idea of "moral desert" (the idea that we should do good for the right reasons, not simply in the hope of being rewarded), it's fairly safe to say that *The Good Place* writers don't agree with Mill. However, it is worth bearing in mind that it can be genuinely hard to be sure what someone's true intentions are in any given case. In a legal dispute or court case we end up having to rely on 1) what happened, 2) what the accused person *says* their intentions were and 3) whether we believe them.

One of the first books Chidi asks his ethics class to read in the good place is *A Treatise on Human Nature.* In this book David Hume argues that there is no such thing as the "self", and that what we think of as the self is merely a succession of perceptions and emotions: "I may venture to affirm of the rest of mankind, that they are nothing but a bundle or collection of different perceptions, which succeed each other with an inconceivable rapidity, and are in a perpetual flux and movement." It is a view that has been compared to the Buddhist denial of the existence of the self.

This "bundle theory of the self" is also relevant when it comes to the question of motivation for "good actions". If we are merely a succession of different mental states, then that makes it all the harder to truly identify what our motivations were for any given action.

Chidi's initial optimism that this book is an easy

starting point for his students is, of course, misplaced, as it turns out that Eleanor really is a bundle of different qualities: it's just that most of them are lazy, thoughtless or unmotivated ones, and she has failed to read the book at all.

Pobody's Nerfect

One of Eleanor's moral epiphanies comes when Tahani tries to help her to bump up her points total by doing good deeds around the neighborhood – she fails to raise many smiles (other than when she tells her "pobody's nerfect" joke at the party Tahani has thrown and everyone thinks it is hilarious). And, more importantly, her points total stays stubbornly the same. It's only when she gives Chidi some heartfelt advice that her total increases. She realizes that she has been doing the right things, but for the wrong reasons (self-preservation). This is the essence of "moral desert": the idea that, as the judge says when they appeal their sentence to the Bad Place, you're supposed to do the right thing because you're a good person, not because you want moral desert (in other words a reward).

Chidi's Challenges

Try testing your moral compass with these quandaries.

1. Imagine that you could raise $2 billion for charity by exposing your flatmate's darkest secrets and selling T-shirts making fun of them. Would you do it?

2. Some scientists claim that we replace every cell in our body every seven to ten years. If Jason isn't the same person as he was at high school, should he still be found guilty of dealing drugs 10 years ago?

3. If you were in a huge amount of pain, would you want a doctor to give you painkillers that made the pain go away but carried a 10% chance of killing you? If not, what percentage risk would you think was acceptable?

What's My Motivation?
Following the Rules

An obvious starting point for moral philosophy is the idea that there are some ethical rules that you just shouldn't break. Whether it be the ten commandments, the golden rule, or basic social etiquette, we do naturally tend to think that some rules are simple and natural. But of course, everyone hates moral philosophy professors specifically because they can rarely agree what those rules actually are . . .

21st Century Dilemmas
Tweet Then Delete
It's interesting to consider the impact that the Internet has had on etiquette and manners. In a world of social media, drunk texting, reality television, flame wars and trolling, have our ideas of personal interactions been degraded from an ethical point of view? Does using text rather than spoken words make us more aggressive and immoral?

The writers of *The Good Place* certainly seem to feel that social media, selfies and the replacement of personal interaction with digital communication has had a detrimental effect – the lists of bad things to do include breaking off from a real conversation to check your phone, and the residents of the Bad Place arrive taking pictures of themselves on selfie sticks as well as being keen to hurry home to watch the rose ceremony on *The Bachelor,* the mere viewing of which can mark up negative points on your lifetime record.

Some of Eleanor's previous bad acts also point to the snares of anonymous and remote interaction with other people. She once posted her sister's credit card details on Reddit, simply because she had told Eleanor she looked tired. When her favourite book (Kendall Jenner's Instagram feed) makes Chidi question whether she is selfish, she responds by suggesting he look at the feed if he wants to see a worse case of self-obsession. And she has also cyberstalked several people, including the hot mailman, using her work account so that it would be "incognito". There is a sense here that anonymity is part of the toxic morality that has grown out of digital communication. And when we see Eleanor reading the magazine *Celebrity Baby Plastic Surgery Disasters* we are also being invited to think that superficiality is only a small step from callousness.

There is a distant echo of this in history. Homo sapiens had violent tendencies from the start, and there were always skirmishes between rival groups. However, true warfare didn't start until the invention of weapons that allowed you to kill someone from a distance, lessening the risk to oneself. And it became more intense as societies developed weapons that were large enough for the rulers to send their armies to war without going to war themselves.

Clearly, we are a species that finds it easier to hurt if we can do it from a distance, without exposing ourselves to risk, and perhaps the Internet is just a reminder of this fact.

As it happens, there are some moral remedies to this problem. When the problem is that you do things secretly, anonymously and from a distance that you wouldn't do openly face-to-face, then two things might teach you to behave more ethically. One is the fear of being discovered – who hasn't observed as a rude email or thoughtless online interaction went viral and thought "There for the grace of God . . ." Would the "world's most selfish bridezilla" have sent texts berating all the guests who refused to pay thousands of dollars for her dream wedding have done so if she taken a bit longer to consider the possibility that she would be mocked around the world for them?

But the trouble is, we never think it will be us that gets caught out, exposed or shamed for our actions.

So how about imagining that every time you go online, there is someone watching you and awarding you points for good, courteous behavior, and docking them for rude, discourteous behavior? Wouldn't that make you think twice before you flamed someone, made up some fake news, went trolling, or gave your sister's credit card details to strangers?

Welcome to the Good Place . . .

The Word of Shawn

Of course, there was a time when many people made this assumption and lived their lives in fear of God. In some ways life was simpler then . . .

Where morality is supposed to be imposed by a deity, this is often called **supernaturalism**. In the Good and Bad Places, Chidi, Eleanor and the others are attempting to decipher the rulings of Shawn and the other "superior beings". If God (or a similar being) is the only source of moral rules, then the way to live a good life is simply to live as God wants you to.

The problem is that this means we must rely on revelations from God as to what he wants from us. It also raises the question of which way round "good" works. Is something good because God approves of it, or does God approve of something because he can see it is good?

The Greek philosopher Plato, following in the footsteps of Socrates, suggested that the latter must be true – a thing is good in and of itself and therefore an eternal, good being, would automatically desire it. (Aristotle was

Plato's pupil and took over the famous Academy after his death, which is why Chidi is so gobsmacked when Eleanor asks him who died and left Aristotle in charge of moral philosophy).

In theory we could test whether something was good or not by working out whether God approved of it, but that doesn't really help. And it leaves us wondering, what if everyone down here agreed something was bad but God approved of it? How would that even work?

So, we end up having to rely on the word of God or the word of Shawn or whoever, as it is passed down in religious scriptures or by priests and other religious leaders. And this can lead to dangerous conflicts for philosophers who question whether their interpretation is true or not. Socrates was essentially executed for questioning the gods of Greece and teaching others to think critically about the received ideas of the time.

There is another problem – if atheists have no sound basis for their judgments of right and wrong, why is it that they mostly come to the same conclusions as religious believers (at least on the basic "no-nos" like "don't kill people")? Why does someone like Chidi, who uses reason to understand ethics, have mostly the same sense of virtue as the most fervent Christian in the Good Place? The supernaturalist might argue that the atheist is getting his sense of right and wrong from God, but just doesn't realize it, but this is a rationalization.

At times in history, people have believed that they can have a personal relationship with God. The Heresy of the Free Spirit (for which the church persecuted many believers in the late middle ages) was the idea that meditation and prayer can lead you to a direct understanding of God's will without the need for intermediaries such as priests. Naturally such movements challenged the power of church leaders, who behaved ruthlessly in crushing them.

As civilizations rose and fell and intermingled, it also became apparent that different religions and cultures teach varying ideas of morality and justice. Within the Christian church, sects developed who disputed the official version of God's word, for instance the Cathars, who were ahead of their time in seeing wars and capital punishment as "bad things", contrary to the current thinking of the church. The sense grew that when you got to wherever you went to after you died, you might indeed be met by a celestial being who told you your church had only got it about 5% right.

Over the centuries, people became more reluctant to accept the word of religious leaders who were so wrong about small things like whether the Earth was the center of the universe or not. And, as a result, the philosophers of the renaissance and beyond became braver at trying to work out for themselves what moral rules were and which ones we should stick to.

Fun Fact: **Socrates and the Philosopher King**

Socrates (as described in Plato's writings) was one of the founders of philosophical reason, but some of his conclusions seem remarkably self-serving. He argued that the kind of Reason required to understand the pure form of Good could only be acquired through years of dialectical training. This leads him to effectively argue (in *The Republic*) that the only truly virtuous people are aged philosophers and that if you want a well-ordered society, you need a philosopher to be king. (He wasn't clearing his throat and pointing at himself when he said this, but I think most people got the message).

Is Killing Someone Ever OK?

There are at least two situations in *The Good Place* which revolve around the ethical quandary of whether to kill someone. As well as Michael's plan to kill Derek (during which he feebly argues it should be morally OK to kill someone to make your own life easier), there is the episode *The Eternal Shriek* in which Eleanor tries to persuade Chidi that they should kill Janet. In both cases Chidi is rigidly opposed, on the basis that murder is probably the most famous "no-no". However, there is a trickier debate to be had about the questions of capital punishment and abortion. In these cases, who has the right to decide whether someone lives or dies?

When it comes to capital punishment, you firstly need to consider what the motivation is. Traditional religious codes allowed for *retribution*: for instance, we find the idea of an "eye for an eye" in several ancient texts. But arguments can also be made for the death penalty as a form of *deterrence,* discouraging others from doing the same thing, or a form of *incapacitation* (preventing the murderer from repeating their crime).

Chidi's favourite philosopher, Immanuel Kant, takes an essentially retributive view, which derives from his categorical imperative. He argues that everyone is valuable and worthy of respect for their ability to freely and rationally make choices. He suggests that the murderer has effectively decided that people should be treated the way he treated his victim, and thus we owe him respect and should treat him the exact same way.

There are problems with the straightforward "eye for an eye" approach. For instance, how should we apply this to a murderer who has killed his victim and their family? Should we kill him and his family too? And how come we don't apply the same principle and punish an arsonist by burning down their house, or a swindler by swindling them? There is also something unsatisfactory about Kant's formulation of the retributive principle when it comes to someone who is mentally disturbed when they kill (thus not making a rational decision at all).

Writers such as Hobbes and Rousseau attempted a social contract defense of capital punishment, arguing that when I join society I effectively sign a contract allowing the state to kill me if I murder (in return for the protection I gain from their willingness to do this to those who might want to murder me). We'll look more at social contract theory later, but here the objections tend to be based on questions like "Who would sign a contract consenting to be killed?", "Why didn't I ever get to read the small print in this contract?" and "How come, if we all agreed not to kill in return for the protection of the state, the state is still allowed to kill people?"

Another type of justification comes from the 17th century writer John Locke, who, as an advocate of natural law, held the idea that we have basic human rights that should be respected. When it came to the death penalty, he argued that the murderer had forfeited their right to life when they chose to kill. The objections to this argument are that this could equally be a justification for vigilante killings, just as much as killing by the state, and the danger of allowing that human rights can ever be voluntarily "forfeited".

It's only in the 19th century that we finally find a few more philosophers willing to suggest the death penalty is wrong. For instance, the utilitarian philosopher Jeremy Bentham (who is referenced in *The Trolley Problem* when the trolley car passes a cinema showing the movies *Bend It Like Bentham* and *Strangers Under A Train*). He carried out a systematic review of the advantages and disadvantages of legalized capital punishment and decided that the drawbacks, such as the fact that it is irreversible in the event of a wrongful conviction, outweighed the benefits and it should be abolished.

Breaking the Contract

If you break a phone contract there are penalties to be paid, because you agreed to that when you signed up. But you never actually signed up to the "social contract", so why should you be punished if you ignore it? This is a common objection to the idea of a social contract.

However, there are plenty of things in life you don't sign up for: your body, your existence, your place of birth. Eleanor and Chidi didn't sign up for the idea that their life's actions would be rewarded or punished after death. The whole ethics of crime and punishment is based on society deciding, by one means or another, how to enforce rules that individuals may not ascribe to. So, the more interesting question when it comes to the social contract may be "what sort of rules is it moral for society to have and enforce?" And when it comes to the Good Place, one of the questions we start pondering early in season 1 is whether this kind of Place really is the right way to reward good behavior.

21st Century Dilemmas
The Violinist

The morality of abortion has often been analyzed from the point of view of whether the doctor has the right to take a life. The famous Judith Jarvis Thomson thought experiment known as "the violinist" is an attempt to defend abortion by focusing more narrowly on the rights of the pregnant woman. She asks us to imagine waking up one morning in a hospital bed, connected by machinery to a famous violinist who is unconscious. He or she has a fatal kidney ailment, and the Society of Music Lovers have found out that you are the only person with the right kind of blood type to help her – your blood supply has been connected up to hers, and you will have to stay here for nine months until she is better – if you unplug yourself from the machinery and walk away, she will die.

Thomson argues that, given certain conditions, it is permissible for you to unplug yourself. She has no right to the use of your body and if you allow her to use it by staying, it should be seen as a kindness, not an obligation. If on the other hand you leave, you are not violating her right to life, merely withdrawing the use of your body (which will lead to her death). She is careful to rule out situations such as selfishly motivated abortions during late-term pregnancy by making her objections clear, but in other cases she suggests this shows abortion can be justified.

This way of analyzing abortion has the merit of not making any assumptions about the doctor's role – you may or not be able to find someone to help you unplug yourself, but it is essentially your decision if you do.

The immediate objections to Thomson's argument revolved around the idea that you have been forced into this situation, so it is only comparable to a fetus conceived after rape. In response she offered an alternative version in which you are trapped in a small house with a growing child who will eventually crush you – it has grown from a "people seed" which has blown in on the wind, in spite of your best efforts to put up screens that will keep such

seeds out. The point here is that many abortions happen in situations where people have taken precautions but the precautions have failed.

Some of the other ways that people have argued against Thomson are to suggest that, by voluntarily having sex, you have tacitly consented to the possibility of the "violinist" using your body, or that you now have a moral responsibility to look after it regardless. Philosophers have also focused on the distinction between the fact the violinist is a stranger whereas a fetus is your child, and on the idea that if you unplug yourself you are letting someone die rather than killing them.

What this thought experiment has achieved is to detoxify a highly sensitive subject by placing the exact same moral questions into a different context – by doing this, Thomson was attempting to identify what the actual moral situation is without letting the more emotive aspects of abortion overwhelm the argument.

Of course, you'll know from *The Trolley Problem* episode (see p. 73) that one thought experiment often inspires a thousand variations on the theme. If you read the kinds of philosophy forums which a geeky young Chidi might have frequented, then you'll find people falling over themselves to find new and innovative versions of (or objections to) the violinist or the people-seeds. But if Thomson has at least found a way to focus attention on the question of whether the mother has the moral right to walk away, rather than allowing abortion to remain strictly defined by the moral concept of "murder", then she has perhaps played a part in moving the debate onto a more rational grounding.

The Golden Rule

We've seen how Chidi admires the work of Immanuel Kant. Kant argued that the best moral pick-me-up was deep contemplation of the idea of moral duty, and that this would lead us to desire to be good. At one point we see Chidi enjoying *Groundwork in the Metaphysics of Morals* which, after a more incomprehensible attempt, he explains to Eleanor as a book about how to be good. Kant's writing is heavy going, in truth. Here's a sample sentence:

> For the pure representation of duty and the moral law in general, mixed with no alien addition from empirical stimuli, has, by way of reason alone (which thereby for the first time becomes aware that it can for itself be practical), an influence on the human heart so much more powerful than all other incentives that might be summoned from the empirical field, that reason, in the consciousness of its dignity, despises the latter, and can gradually become their master; in place of this, a mixed doctrine of morals, composed from incentives of feelings and inclinations and simultaneously from concepts of reason, must make the mind waver between motivations that cannot be brought under any principle, and can lead us only very contingently to the good, but often also to the evil.

Yes, that is just one sentence. Sometimes it's easy to understand Eleanor's blank reactions to dusty philosophers, or Chidi's friend in the philosophy department who regarded Kant as a "lonely, obsessive hermit" with no friends.

The categorical imperative has often been described as like Jesus's golden rule – Kant objected to this for abstruse reasons, but it's basically accurate. To explain the terminology – an imperative in Kant's view is a kind of commandment, a statement that something is required. An example of a **hypothetical imperative** would be "If I want some frozen yogurt, I will need to buy it." This would only be important and correct in certain situations, for instance if I didn't have any fro-yo in the refrigerator. A **categorical imperative** is one that is always true: Kant believed that the most important of these was "Act only according to that maxim whereby you can, at the same time, will that it should become a universal law."

Kant was strongly opposed to utilitarian approaches – for instance, he rejected the idea that murder is only bad because it doesn't maximize good and minimize evil. He saw this as a hypothetical justification, while he strongly wanted morality to be based in "pure practical reason". Moral questions should be decided without reference to the finer details of the instance, as moral judgments like "Do not lie" or "Do not murder" are universally applicable.

On this basis he argued that we need a more duty-based, rational approach to ethics. He says that it's not enough to act "in conformity with duty". For Kant it is clear that Eleanor is not "being good" when she attempts to up her points total by going around doing "good deeds": she is merely trying to act like a good person. Fear of retribution isn't, in Kant's view, sufficient motivation for a good deed.

Kant also argued that people should always be treated as ends (goals) in themselves, not as means to our own ends. When Eleanor uses other people as props in her attempts to be good, she is failing in this respect also.

In the end, it is not the fear of motivation that helps Eleanor most in her self-improvement attempts, nor is it Chidi's rather rigidly Kantian views. It is instead the good example she sees in his selflessness in helping her, even though it is to his own personal cost and he would prefer to be rowing a boat while reading French poetry. He doesn't have to help her, but he feels it is his moral duty to do so. And that is a bigger influence on her than the theory.

Ironically, she is thereby living up to another of Kant's pieces of advice, quoted by Chidi – that we have a duty to improve ourselves.

21st Century Dilemmas
Lying to a Murderer

Imagine a man with a gun came up to you in the street and asked where your neighbor was hiding as he wanted to kill him. You happen to know, but should you tell

him? During Kant's lifetime he had a disagreement with the French philosopher Benjamin Constant on this subject. Constant argued that if truth telling was indeed a universal imperative (as Kant claimed) then you would have to tell a killer where their victim was (he was assuming that refusing to answer isn't an option). Kant's answer to this objection was convoluted, but he continued to argue that you should tell the truth, even in this situation. I doubt your neighbor would give you any Good Place points for being a strict Kantian if you did give his hiding place away – even Chidi occasionally brings himself to tell a white lie for the greater good, although it's debatable that Eleanor's argument that snitches get stitches had more impact on him than Kant on those occasions.

The Ethics of Chilling Out and Looking After Number One

Part of Kant's argument for the categorical imperative is that if you can't will your own personal rule of thumb to be a universal law without getting into a logical tangle, then your rule of thumb is proven to be invalid. For instance, if I think "Stealing the contents of someone's lost wallet is OK" then the basic rule is "Stealing is permissible". But the concept of stealing requires the concept of private property and that wouldn't even exist if "Stealing is permissible" was a universal law. So, it is incoherent to believe this should be a universal rule.

He does distinguish duties such as not stealing (which he calls a "perfect duty") from other areas in which you have free choices. For instance, he suggests that "cultivating your talents" is an "imperfect duty" – it would be unreasonable to expect everyone to constantly attempt to do this, but we can nonetheless use pure reason to establish that it is morally a good thing to do. According to Kant, you shouldn't attract blame for neglecting an imperfect duty, but you should attract praise for doing it (as opposed to a perfect duty, which it is always blameworthy to ignore). When Jason spends his time chilling out, crashing his jet ski into manatees, and selling fake drugs to kids at the local colleges, rather than working hard to take his DJ-ing career from "pre-successful" to the point where Mr Music the DJ is known all over Florida, he wouldn't be judged so harshly by Kant, at least for the DJ-ing part.

Two of Kant's examples of imperfect duty are hedonism and charity. To paraphrase his argument in 21st century terms, if a girl who could make better use of her time chooses to watch women's MMA rather than opera, or lazily throw cups on the floor and expect the environmental activist to pick up her trash, then could she will that everyone does the same? His answer is that society could get by if everyone acted in a lazy manner – but in that case there would be no-one to sell the luxuries that this lazy girl is relying on, no-one to make clam chowder and serve the margaritas. On this basis he only classifies avoiding laziness as an imperfect duty.

More controversially, he also classifies charity as an imperfect duty. To some extent, you can see his point – for instance, most of Tahani's charity work is clearly self-serving and designed to win her a place aboard billionaires' yachts or among the women who grace the cover of *International Sophisticate* magazine. However, Kant is taking a broader view and arguing that "helping others" in general is only an imperfect duty. He considers the case of a person (let's call her Eleanor) who sees other people struggling with life and feels no need to help them. For instance, if the manager of a local coffee shop is sexually harassing the staff, but it would be a hassle not to buy her coffee there, is she morally wrong not to join her dorky boyfriend in boycotting the shop and trying to help the waitresses?

Kant argues that it was not illogical to wish that "don't bother to help other people" was a universal law, and that humanity could function if everyone only looked after number one. And he sees it as impossible to will that everyone should always help other people as this would contradict the need each person might have to be helped themselves.

He therefore ends up arguing that we do have some obligation to help others (such as rescuing a child that is drowning, because we should treat the child as an end, not a means). But in general, helping other people is an imperfect duty and we shouldn't attract blame for not doing so. (Try telling that to the dorky boyfriend – I think Kant just ethicsed him in the face).

Chidi's Challenges

Let's check if you've been paying attention with a few questions . . .

1. Are there any absolute moral rules that you think apply in every single situation?

2. Imagine Eleanor has been surgically attached to a violinist. She can detach herself at any time, but they will die. They insist on playing their violin loudly all day. What should Eleanor do?

3. Suppose there was a way of bringing someone back to life but only if you take the life of another human being. Would you bring a murder victim back to life by killing their alleged murderer? What percentage certainty would you need regarding the guilt of the alleged murderer?

The Trolley Problem
The Trouble With Thought Experiments

One of the joys and frustrations of ethics is that we can almost always show that there can't be a single "right answer" to a problem. We've talked previously about the question of whether a judge should condemn an innocent man to prevent rioting that would otherwise break out and lead to more deaths. Philippa Foot was originally discussing this problem when she first wrote about the notorious trolley problem in 1967 (although versions of the same problem had previously been discussed by philosophical and psychological writers). The basic set-up is that you see a trolley which is going to hit five people and kill them, but you have charge of the lever which you can use to switch onto an alternative track where it will only kill one person. The problem is initially interesting because it explores how willing we are to intentionally kill someone as opposed to letting them die.

Of course, there are many variants on the problem, a few of which Michael forces Chidi to experience himself in the episode named after this thought experiment. The addition of realistic blood and gore certainly adds some urgency to the increasingly absurd variants Michael conjures up.

Forking Philosophers!

It's worth remembering the subtle punishment that the Bad Place has reserved (according to Michael) for philosophers: they are made to go to school naked every day before taking an exam in a subject they haven't studied (and then, less subtly, pounded with hammers). Michael's decision to torture Chidi is largely inspired by his boredom in the ethics classes he has been forced to attend. Many philosophy students will recognize his apathy and irritation, particularly when it comes to the variants that they will almost certainly be taught on this famous problem.

For instance, we are asked to imagine that instead of pulling a lever, we must push a fat man off a bridge to stop the train. Then, imagine that the fat man is the villain responsible for trapping the five victims on the train. Now imagine that instead of a trolley, you are a doctor treating a healthy patient who has organs that could be the only chance of life for five other patients – should you kill him to save their lives? Now if we go back to the trolley problem, how about you can stop the trolley by crashing an empty trolley into it, but then the empty trolley will roll down a hill next to the track and kill a man sunbathing in his hammock in his back yard.

Confused yet?

But the thing is, each of these variants really does bring out some subtly different responses. When asked, more people are prepared to pull a lever than to push the fat man off a bridge (presumably because it seems more personal and direct). The people who are prepared to push the fat man are not always prepared to kill the man in the yard (because he seems somehow to be "unconnected" to the original problem and thus an innocent victim).

There is an additional problem: when the trolley problem is run as a real time experiment, meaning that people must make this decision (as Michael forces Chidi to do, although Chidi's indecisiveness makes it horribly difficult for him), their responses don't always match up to the answers they give to a hypothetical question. Psychologists have suggested that this is because we use a different decision-making process – a slow rational consideration of the factors means people will weigh up the factors and reach a utilitarian decision, aiming for the greatest good and the least harm, even if this is inconsistently applied. But when we must make the decision in a simulation, we have a more instinctual response, and our unwillingness to overcome the taboo against killing means that we often fail to choose the "greatest good" option.

This suggests that ethics and moral philosophy is all very well, but no matter how long you spend pondering the question of "how to be good", your instincts will often take over in real-life situations. This is something Chidi knows from his many awkward moments of indecisiveness in the real world. And it's also something that Michael would have taken great amusement from during his lectures and repeated trips on the trolley of death.

Motherforking Ridiculous!

The trolley problem has become so well-known outside of moral philosophy circles that it has become a popular Internet meme. Aside from the wide variety of versions of the problem thought up by philosophers, there is now a panoply of parodies to choose from, which both celebrate and mock the problem. Here are a few of the most preposterous:

- There's a fat man on the bridge and a fat man tied to the tracks below. If you push one of them on to the other, no-one will die, but five people will go to hell for eternity for watching and laughing. What do you do?

- You are a utilitarian who has been stuck in a time loop, being forced to live the same day 1,000 times each time you make the "right choice". Do you still pull the lever?

- 1,000 people are tied to one track; on the other is a supercomputer that has been working for ten years to find a way to prevent all future trolley problem scenarios from happening, potentially saving many more thousands of lives. Do you destroy the computer or commit mass murder?

- On one track is a worker wearing a T-shirt saying, "Please Kill Me With That Trolley", but it's borrowed from a worker on the other line who has a suicide note in his pocket. However, the note appears to be in the handwriting of the first worker. Which do you kill?

- You're an unemployed moral philosophy professor on the way to an important job interview. If you pause for a moment to pull the lever and save four people's lives, you will miss your bus, and never be employed as an academic again . . .

- There are two pairs of tracks each of which have a fork with five people tied to the tracks, and a fork where one person is tied down. The levers are connected via quantum entanglement, meaning that whichever state one is in, the other must be in the opposite. You don't know where the other pair of tracks is, or even if it is in this universe, but whatever you do six people will die . . .

- Your DNA wants to protect itself. You're strapped to track 1, two of your siblings to track 2, four half siblings to track 3, and eight cousins to track 4 . . .

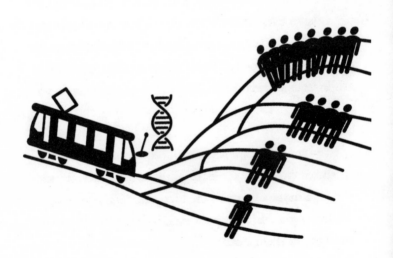

The Baby in the Basement

Given Eleanor's tendency to blame other people (like the dry-cleaner for ripping that dress) or to suggest throwing Tahani under the bus to solve her problems, scapegoating is a regular theme in the Good Place. Michael is another culprit: when Tahani tells him not to blame himself for Janet's murder his response is that he isn't, he is blaming her.

There are some quite complex philosophical problems around the idea of the scapegoat. In the Book of Leviticus from the Old Testament, the chief priest lays all the sins of his people on a goat, and the goat is then driven into the wilderness. The ethical question that most often arises from the idea of scapegoating is how much you would let someone else suffer to guarantee your own happiness (or safety).

In *The Brothers Karamazov* by Dostoevsky, the character known as the "Grand Inquisitor" sets this poser: "Imagine that you are creating a fabric of human destiny with the object of making men happy in the end, giving them peace and rest at last, but that it was essential and inevitable to torture to death only one tiny creature – that baby beating its breast with its fist, for instance – and to found that edifice on its unavenged tears, would you consent to be the architect on those conditions?"

Ursula Le Guin was either thinking of this passage or a similar one in William James when she wrote "The Ones Who Walk Away From Omelas", a short story in which the town of Omelas exists in a permanent state of joyous carnival, where everyone is happy all the time. Everyone, that is, except one miserable child, locked in a room with no love and little food, upon whose misery everyone else's happiness depends. She asks us what the difference is between those who, when they discover the truth, remain in the town, and those who walk away.

Of course, the Christian myth (and many other sun god myths) is based on this basic premise – Jesus suffered, so that we may all go to heaven. Are we benefiting from his misery? Possibly, although as a character in *The Brothers Karamazov* responds to the Grand Inquisitor, there is a big difference when the suffering is voluntary, as it is in the story of Christ.

The philosophical thought experiment of the baby in the basement can be seen as a variation on this theme. Imagine you are in the middle of a civil war and are hiding in a basement with a large group of people. Hostile soldiers are approaching and will discover you and kill you all if anyone makes a noise. A baby starts to cry. The only way to stop it is to smother it or drown it. Could you be the person to do that? (If it helps, imagine that the baby's parents aren't there to protect it).

This is a horrible question to ask. On the one hand,

how could you bring yourself to deliberately kill a defenseless baby? On the other hand, you are all going to die, including the baby, if you don't kill it yourself.

These questions are possibly easier to answer than the trolley problem. In that problem, the person you kill is not already doomed so you really are being asked to choose whether to murder for the greater good. When it comes to the baby in the basement, it is more about the distinction between killing someone and letting them die (and about whether you are willing to sacrifice yourself to stick to the letter of "Thou Shalt Not Kill").

However, it's worth reflecting on how these kinds of set-ups are reflected in the entire moral universe of the Good Place. Right at the start, Michael, the architect of the specific neighborhood in which Eleanor et al live in the Good Place, explains the set-up of the system and how extraordinarily difficult it is to qualify for the Good Place. Which means that almost everyone else you ever knew is going to the Bad Place.

His suggestion that you should not worry too much about that is one of the first moments when viewers might wonder if this is not such a great place as it might seem. It's not just the murderers, the thieves, the molesters and the dictators who go to hell. It's people who read the wrong magazines, supported the wrong football team, liked social media a bit too much, and were lazing around eating ice cream when they could

have been organizing human rights missions to the Ukraine. Only the paragons and saints were rewarded; the medium people like me, and (I'm guessing here) you, have been condemned.

If almost everyone you knew had to go to hell and suffer eternal damnation in order for you to go to heaven, would you be OK with that? Isn't that much worse even than killing that baby in the basement?

Michael Schur, and the writers, deserve huge recognition for how brilliantly and subtly they have woven these kinds of themes into the show. Because part of the underlying message of *The Good Place* is that this is really quite an oppressive system, and the happy few should be able to see that for themselves. If you want to overcome an oppressive system, you need to recognize your own complicity in the way that system is operating. And if the Good Place really required you to be that callous, how could it really be "good" in the first place?

(One of the show's revelations is that there is indeed something wrong with this version of the Good Place. But I can just about avoid that spoiler trap if I say no more at this stage. But the spoilers will probably come more regularly from this point onwards . . .)

Chidi's Challenges

So, what have we learned? Time to ponder a few quandaries . . .

1. If you were given a time machine and went back to 1889, would you be willing to kill the baby Adolf Hitler? (Bear in mind that if you were able to succeed, then you would presumably have to have grown up in a very different world where no-one knew who he was and World War Two didn't happen).

2. Tahani has been given tickets to a lavish charity ball in a country where westerners live a life of constant partying (but the economy is supported by slave labor). Should she accept?

3. Imagine that Chidi has travelled back 150 years in time and finds himself plunged into a trolley problem scenario. The person tied to the track is the grandfather of Philippa Foot (who created the trolley problem) as a young man. If you kill him, the trolley problem will never become famous . . .

What We Owe to Each Other
Rights and the Social Contract

One way of setting up a system of ethics is to start from the idea of human rights. The idea of **natural law**, a basic system of principles for human conduct, goes back to the ancient Greeks. It became highly significant in the 17th century when it was revisited by philosophers such as John Locke – he made the case that people are endowed with certain basic natural rights (which we would call human rights today). In his reading, it is our moral duty to respect other people's rights and the principal moral "no-no" is to violate those rights. This idea was used to suggest that if the government was violating the rights of citizens, then the citizens had the right to overthrow a tyranny – Locke's fundamental rights of "life, liberty and property" were incorporated into the American Declaration of Independence and Constitution in the late 18th century, and the Declaration of the Rights of Man and the Citizen became the founding document of the violent French Revolution.

Your Freedom, My Rights

The main problem with rights comes when we must work out how to balance them. How do we balance the right to property with the right to equality (if, for instance, a small number of people own most of the property)? How does one person's liberty to walk safely down the road mesh with someone else's right to bear arms? How do we balance the rights of a pregnant mother with the rights of her unborn child? How does Eleanor's right to the pursuit of happiness balance with the rights of her drinking pals to expect her to drive them home? And so on and so on.

When it comes to gun control, there are several possible ways of thinking about rights. Firstly, you could argue that there is a fundamental natural right to bear arms. Secondly, you could argue that it is a fundamental right, but only because it derives from the more fundamental right of self-defense (which is more defensible, as humanity didn't always have guns). Thirdly, you could argue that it is a right because the American Constitution (or another country's legal system) says so – here the problem is that you must depend on interpretations of the Constitution, which have varied over the centuries (particularly in how they interpret the small print about a "well-regulated militia"). Fourthly, you could argue that there is no right to own a gun at all.

To make the latter case, you tend to have to rely on

something like the social contract – it's obvious that a person living on their own in a wilderness surrounded by dangerous animals might need weapons, so the objection must be based on how guns are used in real societies rather than in an imaginary "state of nature". Some authors have thus argued that we delegate the right to bear arms to the state, in return for the additional safety that we gain from the relative absence of guns in a society.

You could start a flame war on pretty much any Internet forum in the world by arguing about the rate of gun murder in America (which has relatively little gun control) and Europe (which mostly has strict gun laws). But someone will generally come up with the kind of easy putdown that Eleanor might use in the Good Place: "I didn't sign up for this, so how can this contract be binding on me?"

Perhaps instead it's better to look to two philosophers who question the whole idea of rights. In the period of the French Revolution, the English philosopher Edmund Burke challenged it on pragmatic grounds. No fan of the revolutionaries, he argued that "those who pull down important ancient establishments, who wantonly destroy modes of administration, and public institutions . . . are the most mischievous, and therefore the wickedest of men".

His argument was that the situation of man changes so much over the centuries that eternal principles will never suffice: "All government . . . is founded on compromise and barter. We balance inconveniences; we give and take; we remit some rights, that we may enjoy others; and we choose rather to be happy citizens, than subtle disputants." At the end of season 2 of *The Good Place* it appears the judge who listens to the plea of Eleanor, Jason, Tahani and Chidi may be inching towards a similarly pragmatic view of "eternal laws" and wondering whether more flexibility is required.

Another, more modern critique of rights-based ethics comes from the Scottish philosopher Alasdair MacIntyre who has written that "there are no such rights, and belief in them is one with belief in witches and in unicorns". His basic case is that while philosophers such as Locke thought that natural rights are self-evident truths, all the attempts since to come up with an account of what those truths are have failed because there is no such thing (and different people tend to come up with versions of "rights" that suit their own interests).

What Would Chidi Do?: **The Kingdom of Ends**

Having briefly mentioned social contract theory a few times, let's take a closer look at it. Some conservative thinkers today dismiss it as a way of justifying a powerful state, but some of its origins were closely aligned with the birth of modern democracy. For instance, the French philosopher Jean-Jacques Rousseau argued that we effectively agree to be part of society with a government that is aimed at fulfilling the general will. Under this form of the social contract, everyone would (in his view) be free because they would all give up the same rights and accept the same responsibilities. But the most important thing is that, because no man should be asked to surrender freedom for slavery, he goes on to argue that people should collectively choose the laws under which they want to live.

This brings us to a whole new debate about what kind of democracy would achieve this best. But instead of going there, let's ask a simpler question.

What would Chidi do?

We have a clue here, because in the episode *Chidi's Choice*, Eleanor denies that she is in love with Chidi by listing the things she hates about Chidi, including his glasses that make him look like a cut-price Clark Kent, his many turtleneck sweaters, and his obsession with ethics. Her example for the latter point is an occasion on which Chidi talked about John Rawls for two hours, and only stopped because he noticed she was timing him. After that she smiles at the way he then made fun of himself, and starts rhapsodizing about his twitchy eyebrows, and how kind and patient he is before suddenly realizing that maybe she is in love with him after all.

Anyhow, Chidi's fixation on John Rawls may have partly grown out of his obsession with Kant. One of the formulations Kant came up with for his categorical imperative was the "Kingdom of Ends". He wrote you should "Act according to maxims of a universally legislating member of a merely possible kingdom of ends." This is part of his argument that all moral laws should be universalizable. Since he thinks people should be ends rather than means, he is arguing that we should have moral laws that we would want to have applied to everyone equally.

But how do you go about achieving this, since in real life different people have different vested interests? For instance, someone from a wealthy, privileged background may have a different idea of the relative merits of taxation and welfare to someone from a poor background suffering from disabilities.

One of the more interesting answers to this question comes from John Rawls. He suggests that the ideal way to create a fair set of moral laws would be if all citizens who are part of the society were to get together and decide what the moral laws would be – but they must do this from behind a "veil of ignorance". This means that any of them might end up being born into any level of wealth, any part of that society, any race or gender and so on.

The idea is that this would remove the motivation for people to want self-interested moral laws. So, for instance, in a society where there were slave-owners and slaves, every member of the team making up the moral laws would have to contemplate the possibility that they could become a slave and might end up deciding that slavery should be abolished (without the need for long campaigns and wars to achieve this result). And if everyone had to contemplate the suffering of the poorest in society, there might be a set of moral laws which placed more emphasis on supporting each other.

One problem comes when we try to decide who we include in the jury that is sitting behind the veil of ignorance. Do we include everyone in one country? Or everyone in the world (in which case the inequalities of income between countries become a more pressing issue)? Do we include animals and future people? (See p. 98). The ancient residents of Athens might, for instance, have felt it was fair to include all citizens of their city state, as they did in their Forum, where democratic decisions were made. But in their society, slaves had no rights, and thus weren't included in the decision-making process. Which kind of sucks for the slaves.

And to come back to the Good Place for a moment, what moral laws and rules would residents impose if only the occupants of the Good Place were allowed a vote? Well, you might get a few minor bits of tinkering like "No forking swearing" or "A bit less clam chowder please!" But if you included everyone who might end up in either the Good or Bad Place before they knew where they would end up, wouldn't they vote to abolish the whole bullshirt scheme altogether!?

Tyranny is Generally Frowned On

Early champions of social contract theory like Thomas Hobbes and Rousseau tended to talk about a "state of nature" – a situation before society and the state existed. The social contract was thus depicted as though it were something that people chose at a certain stage of history. What kind of social contract these writers argued for depends on how the writer imagined the state of nature – Hobbes famously saw it as "red in tooth and claw" and thus assumed people would be happy to consent to rule by a tyrannical sovereign in return for escaping it.

Of course, there never really was a state of nature – man is innately a social creature who lived in tribes with various kinds of hierarchy. John Rawls saw his work as a step onwards from classical social contract theory – rather than get bogged down talking about a state of nature, he used the veil of ignorance to ask the question "what sort of society would we want if we didn't know what role we would play in it?"

In the past, social contract theorists were inter-changeably referred to as contractualists or contract-arians. However, these two terms now refer to subtly different traditions, partly due to the work of another of Chidi's favourite authors. **Contractarianism** refers to any theory in which the justification for co-operating with a central state or authority is based in the self-interest of everyone.

By contrast, **contractualism** emphasizes how reasonable or justifiable rules are to other people. Rawls has been described as both, depending on how his work is interpreted. But T. M. Scanlon is generally referred to only as a contractualist.

His book on the subject, *What We Owe to Each Other*, plays an important role in the Good Place. Chidi is a fan, and references it early in the season, as he attempts to teach Eleanor the basic principle that it is good to keep your promises. And it is a page from this book that Eleanor rips out to leave herself a note when she realizes her memory will be wiped. When she finds the message, telling her to find Chidi, she initially wonders what it is (soup?) but the message eventually leads her to her erstwhile and future friend, who only believes her cockamamie story because he sees the page is from the Scanlon book.

Scanlon explores the whole idea of hypothetical consent in a slightly different way. Rather than getting bogged down in trying to define the rights and responsibilities we should agree to, he starts by talking about individuals, and suggests that we owe each other the respect of valuing everyone's point of view. And since the most unique aspect of human existence lies in our ability to assess reasons and justifications, respecting someone as a human must involve recognizing their ability to do that.

Chidi is attempting to teach Eleanor a similar lesson early in season 1 when he tries to persuade her to treat Tahani with respect. Her response is to scornfully suggest that being nice and making friends with Tahani would be playing into her hands as it is clearly what she wants. But as Chidi ripostes, in bemused astonishment, mutual respect is what *everyone* wants.

In Scanlon's system, everyone has a veto over the moral rules and it is only right to do something that no-one could reasonably veto. Eleanor's response to this idea, as explained by Chidi, is to try to fly through a loophole in the system by immediately vetoing the idea that anyone can veto her. This would of course be tyranny which, as Chidi patiently explains, is "generally frowned upon".

Her response also raises the question of how we can sensibly define "reasonable" and "justifiable" without making contractualism a circular theory, which is effectively relying on our intuitions about what is good and fair in order to define "goodness" and "fairness". (Incidentally, "fair" is the word that Shawn sees as the second stupidest human word, after "staycation".)

One advantage of Scanlon's approach is that it is a more flexible and realistic way of understanding how morality works, and why it is subject to a certain degree of compromise and change over time. For this reason, it is a valuable starting point for thinking about how morality works.

There has been some debate about whether his system really is unique and different to the Kantian version of the "kingdom of ends" or even to Rawls. Within the Good Place, however, it plays a big part in Eleanor's attempts to become a good person. When, late in season 2, we see her on Earth, apparently in a timeline where she has evaded death's clutches, she becomes fascinated by an Internet video in which a very serious professor of moral philosophy named Chidi Anagonye discusses the book. (She was prompted towards this by Michael, who quoted the book's title to her: a scene in which Ted Danson is gleefully reprising his role as a bartender from *Cheers*).

In the video, Chidi asks why we should choose to be good if there is no certainty of reward, in this world or the next. He suggests that we make the choice to be good because of our bonds with the people we know and because we naturally want to treat them with respect. He ends by suggesting that none of us are on our own. And if you have seen the episode, you'll know the profound effect his talk has on Eleanor, and what happens next . . .

21st Century Dilemmas
The Deathbed Promise
Promises play an important role in *The Good Place*. Chidi feels obliged to keep his promise to help Eleanor from the start of the show. We know that he is assiduous

at keeping promises: he even missed visiting his mother in hospital when she was having back surgery, because he had promised the nephew of his landlord he'd help him program his telephone. Michael says more than once that you just shouldn't break promises. And Eleanor's more mediocre side comes out when we see that, having promised to take brownies to a baby shower despite her aversion to them, she has been googling good excuses for missing it.

The question of why we should keep promises often comes up in ethics classes. A classic conundrum is the question of why we should keep a deathbed promise, especially if the consequences would be better if you don't. Say you promise your dying grandmother that you will evict her daughter from the house because they have fallen out, when simple kindness dictates you shouldn't go through with it. You aren't hurting anyone by breaking the promise, so should you keep it?

I recently saw a different version of this conundrum on an Internet forum – the poster's wife had died young from cancer, and when she was dying he had spontaneously promised never to remarry. Now, many years later, he was in love with someone, but feeling bound by his promise, even though it was creating a problem his wife probably wouldn't have wished on him in the first place.

What do you think he should have done?

21st Century Dilemmas
Animal Rights

Another early sign that the Good Place may be more complicated than it looks comes when Michael casually kicks a dog into the sun, before explaining that it's OK because it isn't a real dog, and he can make another one to replace it. He describes it as a "construct of a dog" that feels no love, joy or pain (only to have to retract this when its horrified owner asks if that means her dog doesn't love her. This is reminiscent of human attitudes to animals in the past, when they were frequently described by philosophers and religion as having no soul – as being, in Descartes' words, mere automatons).

Our view of animals today is subtler: they are still not generally regarded as "rational agents", but even that distinction is challenged by our modern understanding of the intelligence of animals such as gorillas, dolphins and elephants. And philosophers such as Peter Singer have argued that we should indeed be granting equal moral rights to humans and other animals.

One of the fundamental objections to social contract theory comes from the status of animals. In Rawls' version, rational agents agree the rules behind a veil of ignorance. But who would speak up for animals and at least give them protection from outright cruelty? If we arbitrarily assign spokespeople to look out for them, like lawyers might in a court case, then why should we not grant similar moral status to other speechless things, such as plants, mountains or even bacteria?

Scanlon's version of contractarianism, in which all rational agents negotiate the rules as they go along, and all have the right to veto unreasonable rules, seems more promising on first sight, as we can imagine that people who care deeply about animals will veto rules that hurt the interests of animals. On the other hand, this system relies on the idea that it is unreasonable to impinge on the autonomy of rational agents. This means that no-one should interfere in my business if I am not interfering in theirs, so it is hard to coherently argue that anyone should, for instance, be able to automatically veto my right to eat a bucket of Kentucky Fried Chicken. If the justification is that it distresses them to think of me eating that bucket, then I could make the same argument when it comes to Kim Kardashian West posting selfies on Instagram, but I can't honestly believe I should be able to ban her from doing so, much as I might want to.

Also, if we are giving animals a special status as non-rational agents who should be accorded a moral status, how do we distinguish between animals and non-rational humans, such as the senile or those with severe mental impairment? Surely, we must be cautious about any theory that equates these humans with animals in any way?

Of course, none of this is to say that the champions of these theories don't care about animals, merely that it doesn't really seem to capture our common-sense intuitions about the moral status of animals, and this should make us suspect that it can't be a fully satisfying explanation of ethics.

Chidi's Challenges

Time to wrap your brain cells around these thought experiments . . .

1. When Chidi first summarizes Scanlon's *What We Owe to Each Other* to Eleanor, and explains the way everyone in society can suggest rules, her first thought is that you should get a free ride if your Uber driver talks to you. What would your first suggested rule be?

2. You can delete every single reference to the Kardashians from the Internet, but you'd be breaking a deathbed promise to your grandmother if you did. What is the correct moral choice?

3. Two cages are suspended over a vat of boiling oil. One contains a baby, the other contains ten adorable puppies. Which should you save if you can only rescue one cage? What if the second cage contained 100 puppies? Or 1,000 puppies? What if it contained a single member of a super-intelligent alien species? How do you make the decision and does it depend on whether you are a human, a dog or a super-intelligent alien?

My Best Self
The Ideal of Moral Virtue

In the episode *Best Self* Michael attempts to pull off a Wizard of Oz-style trick by conjuring up a magical golden balloon which the friends can only board if they are the best version of themselves. On each occasion, at least one of the friends fails despite their attempts to support and console one another. Eleanor's realization that her best self might have been the one who was in love with Chidi, in a long-forgotten reboot, is one of the touching moments this provokes (although it is somewhat undermined by Michael's recollection of them rubbing their "food-holes" together).

Of course, this set-up is a clever riff on the whole theme of the show and of ethics in general – surely the whole point of ethics is to be or become the best possible version of yourself. Throughout the show, characters who might once have belonged in the Bad Place are realizing their flaws and working to become better.

But the danger here is **moral perfectionism**, in which you become obsessed with your moral failings rather than focusing on your strengths. Chidi is the sort of person who has spent his life wondering if he is going to be sent to the Bad Place simply because he has almond milk in his coffee, in spite of knowing that it has a negative environmental impact. Tahani, Eleanor and Jason must convince him to stop obsessing over which reboot might have been his best self by reminding him what a positive effect his example has had on them, and inspiring him to forget his self-doubt for at least a few moments. But it's possible that his best self is the one he has yet to discover back on Earth . . .

Devious, Sinister Rocks: **Moral and Intellectual Virtue**

There are times in life when it is easy to give in to paranoia and suspect that all our misfortunes are the deliberate results of external malevolence or that the world is simply "against us". Even inanimate objects can come to seem malign: when Michael is looking for the flaw in his universe in the episode *What We Owe to Each Other,* his first idea is to gather the 78 most "devious, sinister rocks" he can find and ask Eleanor if she thinks any of them are plotting something.

Such questions go back to the dawn of time. If we accept the bible at face value, God's first act after creating the Garden of Eden and placing Adam and Eve in it was to set a deliberate trap for them, sending a serpent to tempt Eve, and placing a beautiful apple as the bait in a trap. Why create a paradise only to find an excuse to snatch it away? He might as well have put a big red button in there with a sign saying, 'Don't Press Me'. Within philosophy one of the most famous thought experiments was from the twisted vision of Descartes, when he imagined that he might be the prisoner of a demon who kept him in a vat while feeding him false dreams of reality (note that *The Matrix* is basically a modern update on Descartes).

In a similar vein, you sometimes must wonder about the motives of moral philosophers. As we have seen with thought experiments such as the trolley problem and the violinist in the hospital, they like nothing better than to imagine a situation in which every possible response can be seen as immoral, and then sit back and challenge their pupils to find the "right solution".

It's sometimes been said that ethics courses are popular with psychopaths who are just trying to find out what "normal" people think is "good". Possibly some of them ended up as professors of moral philosophy.

"Are you going to kill one person deliberately or five people accidentally?" "How many lives would you sacrifice to save your child?" These are dreadful scenarios to dream up, merely to catch out the person who innocently thinks that "right" and "wrong" should be easy to define.

Are moral philosophers trying to prove that morality is impossible? If not, they can certainly give a good impression of it.

What's So Funny About Hell?

The writers of situation comedies can also be compared to malevolent deities, as they put their characters through a series of avoidable indignities and give them tests they are bound to fail. The traditional sitcom, from *Lucille* to *Roseanne* and *Fawlty Towers* to *The Simpsons*, traps a main cast of about four to six characters in an enclosed environment and leaves them to make mistakes, misunderstand one another and be generally tormented with no final resolutions and only occasional respite.

After nine seasons of *Seinfeld* in which Larry David's catchphrase of "no hugs, no learning" left his characters in an eternal loop of weak, lazy, or immoral decisions, the writer finally felt obliged to explicitly recognize the hellishness of their situation: in the notorious final double episode, the four main characters commit yet another minor transgression against moral norms and are imprisoned after a trial in which many of the characters they have wronged come back to publicly denounce them. (It wasn't a popular finale – Larry David went on in *Curb Your Enthusiasm* to put a character playing himself through similar torments before finally righting his own wrong and giving *Seinfeld's* characters a kinder resolution in the show-within-a-show.)

The Good Place falls squarely within the tradition of sitcoms in which a small group of people inflict problems on one another. It even riffs knowingly on *Friends,* when Michael starts to explain friendship in terms of the long-running sitcom. But it has two peculiar virtues: firstly, because the show is set in "the Good Place" and "the Bad Place", where you might expect punishment and reward, this set-up feels natural as well as making it a knowing skit on the usual sitcom tropes. And secondly, this is a show where the main characters genuinely try to learn and do the right thing, while explicitly commenting on the theoretical basis for their actions.

21st Century Dilemmas
Micro Aggressions and Friends

In the episode *What We Owe to Each Other,* we learn that Michael has studied human friendships using the rather bizarre method of watching all ten seasons of *Friends,* puzzling all the while over how Rachel and Monica could possibly afford that apartment in Manhattan.

Our experience of friendship has only got more complicated – in an age where you can get in trouble for having a resting bitch face or giving someone "side-eye", it's all too easy to upset someone. At one point Tahani mentions that her most upsetting moment in life was when her friend Kanye upstaged her good friend Taylor in the process of defending her best friend Beyoncé.

Life is so difficult.

The subject of friendship also raises the question of whether and why it is moral to favor friends over enemies. We'll return to this later, but most psychologists believe it is natural to have some kind of "in-group" and "out-group". The key thing is that seeing the world in terms of "us and them" needn't mean you always see it in terms of "us versus them". Unless of course you are living in a fake paradise explicitly set up to make your life hellish, where all the other people are deliberately tormenting you.

It's not paranoia if they really are out to get you.

Can We Learn to be Virtuous?

In our own lives, we are not usually given impossible dilemmas or deliberately tormented. So why do moral philosophers delight in creating such insoluble situations? The obvious answer is that we are going to face many moral challenges, big and small, throughout our lives: so thinking about the ethics of our decisions can help us learn to make better choices and to understand our motives and consequences.

So, can we really learn to be more moral?

This is a question that was considered by the earliest philosophers: Socrates tried at length to answer it. He concluded rather limply that you probably could learn to be more virtuous, but that the teaching of virtue might not be practically feasible. His successor Aristotle tried to improve on his answer: he suggested a distinction between **moral virtue** and **intellectual virtue.**

Moral virtue is rooted in your habits and disposition: through a combination of how your mind develops at an early age and your early conditioning, you develop what we would call "character" and this affects your intuitions about how to behave.

By contrast, for Aristotle, intellectual virtue is something that can be taught and learned. As you get older, you encounter more complex moral situations, which your early conditioning or genetic make-up haven't prepared you for. By studying history, morals and ethical principles, you can identify the best ways of converting your moral virtue into intellectually virtuous decisions. Once you can do this you have attained **practical wisdom,** which was an important concept for the Stoic philosophers who followed Aristotle.

As we have seen, this kind of virtue-based ethics would be the cornerstone of moral philosophy for many centuries. **Virtue ethics** is a moral system that emphasizes character rather than duties or ethical rules. It essentially suggests that a choice you make is right if it is what a good person would do in the same situation.

As most people aren't saints, virtue ethics tends to take a broader view of a person's life rather than demanding a perfectly right set of choices. This means that being virtuous is a matter of having a set of fundamental values that generally lead you to live and act in the right way. As a system of thought, it comes close to our natural intuition that some people are naturally good, while others can learn to improve their character and decisions. Virtue ethics is also more closely related to the philosophical and religious question of what it truly means to be a human.

Most virtue theorists follow Aristotle in emphasizing that a truly virtuous action is one that comes from rational thought (or intellectual virtue) rather than simple instinct (or moral virtue)[4]. One of the most important modern proponents of virtue ethics is Alasdair MacIntyre, who sums up moral thinking with three questions:

"Who am I?", "Who ought I to become?", and "How ought I to get there?"

(These aren't quite as pithy as Eleanor's three questions to Michael on arrival in the Good Place: all she wants to know is where she is, who he is and what the fork is going on).

There are two main objections to virtue-based ethics. Firstly, it doesn't help us with specific moral dilemmas such as, for instance, whether to legalize euthanasia or same-sex marriage. This is because it rests on a rather circular argument: if being virtuous is simply "acting how a virtuous person would act", then how do we agree what defines a person as virtuous in the first place?

Alasdair MacIntyre, unlike many previous champions of virtue ethics, rejects the idea that we can take a **universalist** view (one in which there are universal

---

4 It's interesting to compare this with social intuitionism (p.178) which suggests all of our actions are based initially on instincts, which we simply rationalize after the event.

principles which define virtue), instead choosing to emphasize the context in which actions take place – both the moment in history and the traditions in which a person has learned their ethical judgments have an impact on what is regarded as "good". One author has summed up MacIntyre's **contextualist** views thus: "Our inability to arrive at *agreed* (rationally justifiable) *conclusions* on the nature of rationality and justice, and issues like abortion and the Vietnam war, should be explained by the fact that we belong to different practices (in his terminology traditions) which embody different and incompatible ideas of rationality and justice."[5]

But this leads on to the second big objection to virtue ethics: if what we consider "good" and "right" changes from time to time and culture to culture, then we have to go into questions of whether virtue is **objective** (in which case how do we judge which era and cultures have the "right" morality?) or **relative** (in which case how can we definitively judge any act or person as being virtuous at all?)

It was because of these objections to virtue-based ethics that most philosophers in recent centuries started to look for alternative ethical systems such as utilitarianism or the social contract.

---

5 Mikael Stenberg, *Rationality in Science, Religion, and Everyday Life.*

Fun Fact: **Michael**

In the early versions of the *The Good Place* script, Michael Schur used "Ted" as the name for Ted Danson's character. However, while he was visiting Notre Dame Cathedral, the tour guide told him about the archangel Michael, "the angel who weighs people's souls and decides whether their souls are good or bad", and the name seemed apposite for the character.

The Balloon Debate

In the final episode of the first season of *The Good Place, Michael's Gambit,* Eleanor and Jason have narrowly missed Shawn's deadline for returning to face the music. The result is a rather arbitrary decision by Shawn that any two out of Eleanor, Jason, Chidi and Tahani must go to the Bad Place, but they have to decide between themselves which two.

This is part of an escalating pattern of events in the Good Place which make us suspect that there is something essentially wrong in the way that the four main characters are being treated there. But it is also the trigger for a balloon debate: these are entertainments in which people debate who out of a group of people deserves to stay in a balloon, and who has to jump out to save the others. They are often held in schools with people playing the parts of historical or fictional characters, with the audience voting on who should be saved at the end.

In this case, the reward and punishment for winning or losing seems extreme – eternal salvation versus immediate damnation. And all the characters make good points about why they deserve to stay or go. It is of course an impossible choice. How do you choose between a perennial ditherer with a good heart, a giraffe-sized clothes horse who raised $6 billion for charity in pursuit of photo-ops, a woman who was raised by two complete dirtbags and failed notably to rise above them in life, and the dumbest DJ in Florida?

An interesting philosophical variation on the balloon debate comes from Garrett Hardin, an American ecologist and philosophy professor. In 1974 he suggested the idea of "lifeboat ethics". Imagine a lifeboat with 50 people in it, and 100 more swimming in the water waiting to be rescued. However, the lifeboat has only got room for 10 more people. How do you decide who to save? If some of the people in the boat are old, sick or dying, should they should be thrown overboard to rescue fitter individuals with a better survival chance?

Hardin used this thought experiment as an analogy for the ecological and economic state of the world. The 50 people represent the developed nations, while those in the water represent those in the poorest countries.

Resources are divided unequally and there are decisions to be made in the future which will affect the survival prospects of millions. Hardin's aim was to criticize the idea that perpetual economic growth is a good aim for humanity – on this basis he rather harshly suggested it might be best to let no-one in to make sure the lifeboat's buoyancy was sustainable. He compared his "lifeboat ethics" to "spaceship ethics" in which we treat the planet as a vessel we all share, so we should make life as good as possible for as many people as possible. However you react to it, the scenario raises interesting ethical problems.

We know Eleanor isn't a great fan of environmentalists – in the first episode after she has discarded her plastic cup on the ground, she tells the earnest young man who points this out to pick it up himself if he is so "horny for the environment". It is largely to emphasize this failing that Michael ironically congratulates her on great work she has done saving the planet at the start of season 2 (and it is also to her credit later in the season that she finally develops a conscience on this subject).

A later adaptation of the lifeboat problem focuses attention even more on the different ethical dilemmas it raises. In this version we are to imagine a sinking ship with ten passengers and a lifeboat that will only fit six of them. The ten passengers are a woman who is pregnant; a lifeguard; a young married couple; a pensioner with fifteen grandchildren; a young teacher; ten-year-old twins; an aged nurse; and the ship's captain. Each is selected to bring out different aspects of why we would make choices based on the usefulness of each passenger during the journey, their life expectancy, how many people rely on them, and so on. Each selection procedure might be deemed rational and ethical to some while others would choose differently.

Most actual balloon debates are won by the funniest, most charismatic speakers. And in the case of the Good Place, (spoiler alert!) while we are gradually realizing that all of the four friends have faults, it is the fact that we have come to like them as individuals that makes us feel none of them deserves to be condemned to the Bad Place.

Which is why the denouement of this episode is such a stunning dramatic moment . . .

21st Century Dilemmas
First World Ethical Problems

We come to like Tahani in the first instance because, while she is self-absorbed and privileged, she is shown feeling inferior to her even luckier sister. Compared to most people, Tahani clearly has very little to feel bad about; she has had a highly privileged life, and even starts out with the grandest home in the Good Place. But we end up empathizing (slightly) with her when she is forced to live in a smaller house and to wear cargo pants (which she describes as making her look like a female plumber, before wondering what the correct name would be for that: "toilet sweep" or "clog wench"). OK, maybe she loses our sympathy again when she describes the pants as surprisingly comfortable and then wonders what has gone so wrong in her life that she is saying something positive about "off-the-rack separates".

The question raised here is how context affects our view of ethical situations. In the media, news from our own country is given higher priority than stories from other countries. Up to a point that makes sense, since we care more about those closer to us than those far away. But how about the calculus that has been cynically described as meaning that one western life = ten third world lives? When it comes to the reporting of tragedies and disasters, why do we have so much more regard for those who live in similar circumstances to ourselves?

This is partly about how we define "us and them" or the in-group and the out-group. Some people might only include people from the same income bracket, political persuasion and area as being "us". Others would want to try to extend the concept of "us" to all humans or to all thinking creatures, although this can be a difficult thing to truly achieve.

The definition of in-group and out-group has a

major impact on how ethical theory is interpreted in practice. If you are a fan of utilitarianism or any brand of consequentialism, you must work out how wide to spread the net for possible consequences of your actions. Should you consider people not yet born, people in other countries, animals, or plants? The calculus of your decisions feels very different if, for instance, you consider that a discarded plastic bottle may eventually end up as lethal plastic fragments in a distant ocean.

We saw how the same problem affects social contract theory – you need to work out who you are going to count if you are to come up with rules of morality from behind a veil of ignorance (Rawls), or through ongoing negotiation (Scanlon).

On one level ethics is easy to define. We all know that Chidi is right when he says that forgoing something you enjoy (like being able to fly) to do something for the greater good (like picking up the trash) is a basic, moral "yes". However, we also value loyalty: we want our friends and family to be on our side, and to be willing to turn a blind eye to our faults. It's easy to ethically deduce that capital punishment is wrong, but if someone close to you is murdered, your instinct may well be to want the murderer killed in revenge. And we all know that stealing is wrong, but most of us would nonetheless see stealing something from a rich corporation as "better" than stealing from an old lady or local store.

One answer to the question of why ethics professors rarely give us a simple answer is that ethical flexibility is both unavoidable and, in some respects, necessary. Peter Singer has said that "tradeoffs are essential, because virtually nobody is a saint". We make constant tradeoffs in our judgments about ethics. It is instinctive behavior for us to take the side of those closest to us, which is the point of Jesus's story of the Good Samaritan. In this parable he is advocating the more difficult act of being good to strangers and outsiders.

This is something that many people might regard as an acid test of "good behavior". How do you treat the underprivileged in society, the ones that you could "get away" with ignoring or treating badly? Are you nice to your family but rude to strangers? Do you tip the waiting staff in a restaurant or send wine back just to piss them off? Since you have nothing to gain from treating them well, we assume that the Good Place points system should reward you for decent, civil behavior towards those people.

This is also where Kant's categorical imperative or Jesus's golden rule can be a useful yardstick. If you treat someone how you would want them to treat you in the same situation, how far can you possibly go wrong?

Tribal Epistemology

The question of the in-group and the out-group is obviously a huge factor in 21st century politics, especially in the deepening divide between conservative and liberal views in the USA and related schisms around the world. The notion of "tribal epistemology" has been invoked to describe the way that people seek out information and news (even "fake news") that confirms their biases. Many news stories these days fuel endless raging debates in which people are more concerned about scoring points than being good or truthful. The real danger comes when we go so far into tribal behavior that we demonize members of the other group and see them as enemies. When we are morally outraged by a point of view we are more willing to believe bad things about the people who hold that point of view. Again, we can turn to two of Chidi's favorites for advice on how to counter this tendency. Kant wrote that we should treat every person as an end, not a means – in other words we should accept that they are different to us with their own motivations and perceptions, and we should not exploit them. While Scanlon's whole contractarian philosophy is rooted in the simple idea that it is wrong not to respect others so that we should take everyone's view into account when deciding how to act.

Chidi's Challenges

Time to check what we've learned so far . . .

1. Descartes imagined being the prisoner of a demon who kept him in a vat; *The Matrix* similarly imagines that machines are feeding us a false reality. If Jason was in a simulated reality, how would he know?

2. Eleanor can abolish world poverty and disease, but she would have to spend every waking hour of the rest of her life watching the ten series of *Friends* on a constant loop. What should she do?

3. If four professors of moral philosophy were in a balloon and it was going to crash into the ocean, would you bother saving them?

Existential Crisis
Alternative Approaches to Ethics

A large part of Eleanor's motivation in life was wanting to be "left alone". We see her refusing a job at a large corporation where she would have had to join in with company bonding exercises, instead accepting a job selling fake medicines to the elderly where at least she won't be coerced into befriending people. She does have some drinking buddies but manages to alienate them through her reluctance to be the designated driver.

However, we come to realize that at least part of the reason for her solitary nature is her awful childhood. Her parents were self-centered and thoughtless. Her mother's botched attempt to tell her the family dog has crossed a long rainbow bridge to a lovely farm quickly deteriorates into an admission that the dog is in a duffel bag under the porch, having been left to die in a hot car. Her stoner dad used her college fund in an attempt to frame her mum's ex-boyfriend. Neither of them seems remotely bothered when Eleanor's eventual response to an awful childhood is to legally separate herself from them. Indeed, they are so awful that we can understand Eleanor's suspicion that they might be in the Bad Place being put to use torturing each other.

Fun Fact

Eleanor is so good at selling dodgy medicine that she proudly boasts to Chidi that she was the top sales person five years running: Chidi is even more aghast that she doesn't immediately seem to realize that this makes her sins worse, not better. Of course, Eleanor is still under the impression that moral imperfections can include being a "chunkster" so her moral compass has a long way to go at this stage.

Hell Is Other People

We can understand that Eleanor came to agree with the famous Jean-Paul Sartre quote: "Hell is other people." But what we come to realize through the first season of *The Good Place* is (spoiler alert!) that this whole set-up is very similar to the Sartre play *No Exit*. In the play, three characters who expected to be in hell find themselves locked in a room together. Each of them aggravates the others, and they all find themselves being driven mad, with no way to escape. The play suggests that this would be a very severe form of hell.

At the end of season 1 Eleanor realizes that what they

have been told is the Good Place is the Bad Place. Chidi, Tahani, Jason and herself have been hand-picked by Michael for their ability to drive the others to distraction. They are being made to punish each other for their sins. Maybe we should have guessed right at the start, because no-one truly expects heaven to serve an endless diet of frozen yogurt, do they?

Of course, what Michael couldn't have anticipated is the degree to which the four of them have bonded and even helped one another to become better people. He expected Chidi to try and teach Eleanor "good person" stuff, just not that she would learn anything. And the ways in which she has become better aren't purely down to moral desert or fear of punishment. She really has learned part of what it takes to be a good person. We end up feeling that, given a better start in life, she might not have ended up being the immoral dirtbag she clearly was.

Maybe . . .

I dimly remember a childhood sermon at the local Catholic church – the priest was describing someone arriving in hell, where all the forks had impossibly long handles and no-one could eat the lovely food on offer, no matter how hard they tried to feed themselves. By contrast, in heaven, the same forks were being used but the people there were happily feeding each other. The point of the story (and one of the morals of *The Good Place*) is that there is no such thing as hell or heaven, just people and how they choose to treat each other.

By seeing how Chidi behaves, and learning "what we owe to each other" from his example, Eleanor has started to learn how to be a good person against all the odds. We saw in the last section how morality is affected by how broadly we define our "in-group". Ethics is largely about the question of how we balance our self-interest with the wider good. The way that our morals are rooted in our interactions with other people can be seen as the dividing line between various types of social contract theory, and (arguably) left- and right-wing politics.

But the very first step to be taken is to care about other people at all. Eleanor's in-group has, for most of her life, been herself. Ironically, being put in the Bad Place has started to teach her how she might deserve to be in the Good Place. In the episode . . . *Someone Like Me as a Member,* she explains that she is a different person because of people like Chidi who have helped her and this has inspired her to want to be more like him.

Or more like a less indecisive version of Chidi. Because it is also at this stage of the story that we start to see more clearly what Tahani and Chidi have done to deserve damnation – her good deeds have only been done for the worst of reasons, while he has tortured those around him with his dithering and moral perfectionism.

So, *The Good Place* is brilliantly playing out one of the central themes of ethical philosophy. In the book *What*

We Owe to Each Other, Scanlon starts from the idea that we must respect each other as individuals and that all wrong deeds spring from a failure to do so. In *The Good Place* we have seen four individuals learn increasingly to care about one another and to be more selfless.

And this is what drives the narrative of the whole show, the question of how much Eleanor (or anyone) can truly change. In keeping with this theme, season 3 starts out by looking at the question of whether Eleanor could indeed become a good person in the real world, given a few nudges in a better direction.

Swipe Right: **Do Soulmates Exist?**

Another driving theme of *The Good Place* is whether we really have a soulmate (as Michael suggests in the initial episode) and whether Chidi and Eleanor might be an unlikely example. Plato wrote precisely about this idea in *The Symposium,* where he has the dramatist Aristophanes utter these words: "Love is born into every human being; it calls back the halves of our original nature together; it tries to make one out of two and heal the wound of human nature. Each of us, then, is a 'matching half' of a human whole . . . and each of us is always seeking the half that matches him." Which is surprisingly close to the cliché of Hollywood love, for an ancient philosopher. We can see that Eleanor seeks Chidi out, time after time, and asks him to help her. We also know that (as Michael tells us) he never refuses to do so. And we know that there is at least one timeline in which the two are happily in love and willing to admit it. What we don't know is what lies at the end of their story.

I Have Been Murdered!

After the accidental-on-purpose killing of Janet, Eleanor's post-hoc rationalizations of the crime (combined with her blaming Chidi and begging him not to confess, no matter how strong his urge to tell the truth) raise the question of whether killing someone deliberately is the same as letting them die or killing them accidentally (the consequences being identical). But they are also a messy example of how we often behave in practice. Rather than calmly coming to rational judgments, and making all our decisions based on moral laws, we often muddle through, making it up as we go along and justifying ourselves after the event.

At least, this is the main argument of the **social intuitionist** model of morality in which the reasons and rationales beloved of moral philosophy professors aren't the real reasons for our decisions (which are instead based on emotional intuitions in this theory). The theory is rooted in the field of psychology rather than philosophy but is worth mentioning as a challenge to the entire project of philosophical ethics.

Earlier psychological models did take a **rationalist** approach, which is closer to traditional ethics – this assumes that we make rational decisions about what is good and bad and try to apply this in life. Social intuitionists disagree with this – they argue that our moral judgments are, in the first instance, intuitive (or even subconscious), and that we rationalize them after the event. They believe that when we do put forward moral judgments, it is mainly as a way of influencing other people to agree with us (or of disputing their moral judgments).

So then, our conscious thought processes about morality are merely post-hoc justifications. Jonathan Haidt, one of the main proponents of this theory, points to studies of "moral dumbfounding" in which people have a strong ethical gut reaction to something but are unable to come up with any rational explanation as to why. For instance, if we are told that a brother and sister have been sleeping together and don't regret it, we tend to have a strong repulsion, but we can't come up with a watertight explanation for why. The argument is a bit more complex – social intuitionists argue that we do have subconscious "heuristics" (guides to action and morality) which will be reflected in our reactions to events. But they also suggest that when we attempt to explain the thought process that led to a moral reaction, we are often unaware of or untruthful about the actual causes.

Haidt does acknowledge that moral reflection and interpersonal discussion of ethics can create new intuitions. We might, for instance, become more accepting of incest or of gun control if we have discussions or private reflections on events that lead us to reconsider our previous intuitions. However, when we apply these new intuitions, the same process will be in evidence – the intuition will lead to the judgment, which we will then come up with a rational explanation for.

Professors of moral philosophy need not completely despair when confronted with this psychological theory – they might choose to believe that the interpersonal discussions and private reflections are of more significance than the social intuitionists suggest, but both camps do at least recognize that thinking about ethics can lead us to form new judgments and to behave differently in future.

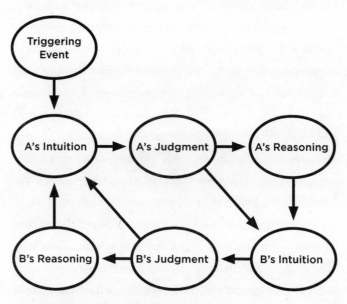

A visualization of the social intuitionist model.

Fun Fact: **A-B-Janet**

One example of how our intuitions take over from our rational thoughts comes when Chidi and Janet try to press Janet's red button and murder her. In spite of her specific warning that she has a failsafe system of pleading for her life, their instincts cut in when she pathetically begs to be allowed to live. Even after she admits that the picture of three children she has shown them (including little Tyler, who is fighting his asthma "like a champ") is a stock photo, they find it hard to go through with the deed. The fact that this is exactly the sort of stunt that the makers of a TV show would pull to tug our heartstrings only makes the joke funnier.

Michael's Existential Crisis

When Chidi attempts to teach Michael about ethics, the first problem is that Michael simply doesn't understand life from the point of view of a mortal. However, when Chidi manages to force Michael to confront the fact that he too may eventually cease to exist, he provokes a serious existential crisis in his student. Michael starts to see everything as pointless, parties as just a distraction from the horrors of a universe that is empty, indifferent, and going through an inevitable process of entropy and decay.

A similar view of the universe lies at the heart of existentialist thought. Thinkers such as Albert Camus and Jean-Paul Sartre see the universe as essentially meaningless, and this leads them to emphasize our freedom to choose. In the latter's *Existentialism and Humanism* there is a story about a student who, during World War II, asked Sartre whether he should go to England to fight with the Free French Forces or stay in France to care for his elderly mother. Sartre's response was "You are free, so choose."

Some people dismiss existentialist ethics as a kind of moral subjectivism in which no moral statement is objectively true. But it's a bit more subtle than that. Where some ethical theories such as Kant's or utilitarianism suggest there is a foundational method of deriving all moral principles, existentialists suggest that moral values can't be reduced to one set of rules, and there will be situations in which different choices hold different moral pluses and minuses. What Sartre was emphasizing to his student was that rather than looking to philosophy for the answer to his question, he should recognize that the meaninglessness of the universe meant that he had the ultimate power and responsibility – he had to make the choice himself and live with the consequences.

In general, the fact that we are mortal and that life will end has a huge influence on our perceptions of morality. We don't have an unlimited amount of time to decide what the right way to behave is, and rules such as "Thou Shalt Not Kill" have a fundamental role in our ethical framework.

Happily, Michael skips from his existential crisis right into a healing mid-life crisis: he acquires a sports car, a flashy suit and persuades Janet to be "Jeanette", a glamorous blonde who laughs at all his jokes. Possibly not the most ethically sound approach, but it is one way of coping – and it does achieve what Chidi has said that Michael needs, which is to recognize that life is absurd and to find a way to confront and deal with that absurdity.

Talking About Television

One minor theme of *The Good Place* is the self-referential nature of some of the humor. Eleanor refers to Michael as the man who invented this universe, and he can often be seen as comparable to a show-runner like Michael Schur.

We see Vicki and Michael struggling to keep control and bickering over plotlines, as though they are struggling to keep a show on the air. Michael talks about the pressure that maintaining the show's storylines puts on him and berates the demons for their stupidity in carrying out his instructions (like the hot mailman Chris, who interrupts every conversation with Eleanor

The Good Place

by removing his shirt and running to the gym).

Even Vicki's rage at being given a minor role after the reboot is couched as an actress's diva-ish complaint – she pouts that you wouldn't keep a Ferrari in the garage and goes on to affect a ludicrous limp and backstory in an attempt to keep the limelight she was enjoying as "Real Eleanor". This is a TV show that knows it is a TV show and isn't scared to make fun of itself on that basis.

Chidi's Challenges

Just to make sure you've been paying attention, here's your homework . . .

1. A perfect algorithm has been developed that can identify your soulmate, but it turns out he or she is married to a stoner and living in a trailer park in Arizona. Do you have their partner framed so you can live the rest of your life happily ever after with them?

2. You get your dream job, but the company rules are that you have to go on bonding exercises every week night. What do you do?

3. Someone is threatening to hurt your child. Your instinct is to kill them, your rational response is to call the police even though there will be a two-hour delay. Which do you do?

Team Cockroach
The Ethics of Behaving Badly

When Eleanor's selfish actions (stealing shrimp, calling Tahani a giraffe, choosing flying over clearing up the trash) start destabilizing the neighborhood, the results are highly visible – the nightmarish sequence with the flying shrimps and giant frog, the trash storm itself and the huge sinkhole that opens up in the neighborhood.

Unforeseen consequences are a bit of a nightmare, not just for Eleanor, but for ethics in general. The whole branch of consequentialist thought that includes utilitarianism has a problem – since we can't always know what the result of our actions will be, how can we possibly base our morality on the consequences, rather than on the act itself or our intentions?

The Samaritan's dilemma is based on the idea that acts of charity have unknowable consequences. If we provide help to someone, for instance by providing them with food when they are penniless, there is an argument that they may come to be dependent on that help and unwilling to find alternative solutions. This argument is often used (for instance by the free-market economist

James M. Buchanan) to argue against charity, as well as "organized charity" such as welfare and foreign aid. It has also been used to argue against communism and socialism, on the basis that any kind of state aid suffers from the same problem: people and industries become dependent on it rather than finding better solutions.

There is an alternative way of viewing the conundrum, which is to argue that the Samaritan's dilemma should focus our minds not just on whether to give money to people in need, but how we do it – if we are enabling the needy to avoid finding other solutions, we may be doing more harm than good, whereas if we can find constructive solutions then we may be avoiding that theoretical harm.

In short, if you buy someone a fish, you feed them for a day; if you buy them a fishing rod, you feed them for a year.

The other main objection to the Samaritan's dilemma is that it makes the very strong assumption that there are other better options available. As people found out in the Great Depression, or after Hurricane Katrina, that ain't necessarily so: people who are helped for a period of time when there simply aren't other options won't necessarily turn down better options when they do eventually come along.

Fun Fact: **Annoying Behavior**

In an interview, Michael Schur, who created *The Good Place*, said the idea for the show came from his drives around L.A. during which he observed "a lot of annoying behavior, as you do". He started playing a game with himself where, for instance, someone lost eight points if they rudely cut in on him in traffic. "And I thought what if it's a game and the people with high scores get into the Good Place and people with the lowest scores get into the Bad Place."

Almond Milk and the Slippery Slope

Chidi's aversion to lying and making quick moral decisions imply a fear of the **slippery slope** (also known as the thin end of the wedge or the camel's nose in the tent) – this is often used in moral arguments to imply that a minor moral dilemma or transgression might lead to greater ethical danger. For instance, if we allow voluntary euthanasia, are we on the slippery slope to legalizing involuntary euthanasia? And if Chidi allows himself to have almond milk in his coffee, despite knowing the environmental consequences, is he on a slippery slope to drinking cow's milk, eating inappropriately sourced avocados or quinoa from countries with poor human rights records, or even buying his coffee from a café where the owner is known to have harassed the waitresses?

In short, is he on the highway to hell?

It's important to differentiate between a slippery slope event and a slippery slope argument. A slippery slope event is a situation in which one thing leads to a chain of causation with larger consequences. Whereas the expression "slippery slope argument" is generally used to suggest that an argument that relies on the inevitability of such a causal chain is fallacious.

Consider this argument – a mother is worried that if her teenage boy starts hanging out playing pool at the youth club, he is more likely to start smoking and drinking. She is worried that this will lead on to him trying cannabis and that from there it's inevitable he will be tempted to try harder drugs. Her worry is that the pool playing is the slippery slope event. But if her friend tries to persuade her that she is being too alarmist, they might tell her that she is making a "slippery slope argument".

Slippery slope arguments are often used in fearmongering. A newspaper columnist might argue that if we legalize cannabis, we are on the way to treating heroin as morally acceptable. Or that allowing cars to drive at higher speeds on rural motorways will lead to more deaths from dangerous driving on urban roads.

When objecting to a slippery slope argument, you can invoke the continuum fallacy. This is the often fallacious idea that there is no "middle ground". For instance, if Chidi drinks and enjoys his almond milk, he might possibly stay there on the middle ground of doing something "a little bit wrong" but not progress to greater levels of liberal faux pas.

It's interesting to note a couple of alternative ways of thinking about slippery slopes. In his book *Attacking Faulty Reasoning*, T. Edward Damer prefers to talk about the domino fallacy, to draw attention to the idea that

there is a causal chain at work here, and that, to accept the slippery slope argument, we need to be certain that each and every domino will indeed knock down the next. Meanwhile, German writers tend to use a different metaphor for the same concept, talking more often of a dam bursting when there is too much pressure on it – this is an interesting variation because it doesn't imply a chain of events, just a big consequence from a small change (for instance a rise in the water level).

To assess a slippery slope argument, we need to be careful about the logic involved. Generally, there is an event, A, which seems inconsequential. And there is an outcome, Z, which would be a much more serious issue. To work out whether the argument has any validity we need to know whether it is inevitable that A will cause Z, or at least whether there is a reasonable, calculable probability that A will lead to Z. Slippery slope arguments get much of their power from the implication of inevitability, so by analyzing them in terms of probability we remove some of that spurious power. For instance if A is "Chidi drinks almond milk" and Z is "Chidi ignores evidence of sexual harassment", we might argue that there is actually close to 0% chance of this happening because Chidi's sense of moral outrage is so well developed that he will never get to Z. Whereas if A is "The construction company use cheap cement" and Z is "The dam eventually bursts", there might be something closer to 100% probability in which case a warning that the construction company shouldn't cut costs is entirely valid.

Moral Relativism and the Majority View

At various points of time, some thinkers have argued that morals are relative, rather than absolute. This means that they depend on the person, the culture, or the time period in question. You can take a variety of moral relativist positions. For instance, you might argue that, when people disagree on ethics, neither is objectively right. Or you might take this further and argue that because no-one is objectively right, we must tolerate other people's behavior even if we disagree with their morals. But there are some obvious problems with moral relativism. If morals aren't objective, but relative, then are we forced to say that the majority view is always right? This would mean that Eleanor was a bad person when the group believed her to be but became a good one at a later point. And it could be taken to mean that the people who opposed slavery in the 18th century were simply wrong, while the slave-owners were acting morally correctly. It is because most people find it hard to truly act on the assumption that morality is this flexible that we end up trying to find better ways to describe our moral judgments. We might believe, as David Hume did, that the universe doesn't care about "good" and "bad": but we still want to be able to articulate the very human belief that good and bad do matter.

Chidi's Challenges

1. Tahani finds out her family fortune was earned in the slave trade in the 18th century. How much of her personal share should she give to charity before the moral scales are even?

2. You are homeless and hungry. A passing economist explains that they aren't going to help you out because it will encourage you to be dependent on charity. What do you do?

3. Chidi finds out that blueberry harvesting involves cruel working practices. Should he still buy a blueberry muffin in the morning?

. . . Someone Like Me as a Member
Moral Particularism and Egoism

You may have noticed that the overview of the terrain of ethics that we provided at the start of this book wasn't completely comprehensive: it didn't include every possible way of thinking about morality. Sorry: it is simply too complex a subject to be reduced to a single page map. One moment in *The Good Place* that introduces us to a radically different aspect of ethical thought comes in the Bad Place, when Chidi is deeply concerned about having to tell a lie. When he keeps citing absolute Kantian moral principles, Eleanor's reply astonishes him by revealing that she has been reading on her own and is familiar with the **moral particularism** espoused by Jonathan Dancy, despite Chidi never having covered it in his lessons.

Thinking Outside the Bun

Eleanor's (and Dancy's) suggestion is that there are no absolute moral rules. Nothing is absolutely good or bad regardless of the particular situation. Where deontology tries to extrapolate strict rules, and consequentialism implores us to consider the consequences of our actions, particularism takes a different road. It sees all moral knowledge as being about moral rules of thumb, and of previous solutions and their outcomes. If we act in good faith, without narcissism, to do what we believe is good and right, then we are acting morally according to a moral particularist.

Eleanor's instant decision that she is a moral particularist now is largely designed to pressure Chidi into forgetting his Kantian purity for a moment and lying his ass off to save them from being revealed to the actual demons that they are surrounded by. But it seems a fairly accurate label for the sort of moral views she is maturing into. She hasn't learned how to be a good person by taking on board all of Chidi's absolutist principles, but by observing him being good. Personally, she is more flexible and can see that this is a moment when "lying is always bad" isn't a helpful rule of thumb.

Moral particularism can be described as a form of **situational** ethics: the wider school of thought that there are no absolute rules and we need to take context into account in making moral judgments. This is the position of some existentialist philosophers (such as Simone de Beauvoir) as well as liberal Christian theologians including Dietrich Bonhoeffer, the prominent German Christian writer who was brave enough to stand up to Hitler and publicly denounce him (and was executed for his courage – don't make the mistake of believing that you can't be a moral particularist and still be a good person).

It's worth noting that the law often works in practice as though it is taking a moral particularist view. For instance, Justice Stephen Breyer, from the Supreme Court in the USA, was once discussing bright-line rules, which are clearly defined standards in American law designed to leave little room for interpretation. He commented that "no single set of legal rules can capture the ever-changing complexity of human life". In practice, the work of higher courts in America and elsewhere is often aimed at weighting a complicated set of issues and trying to come to a balanced view that isn't constrained by such absolute principles.

Fun Fact: **Kristen the Philosopher**

Kristen Bell, who plays Eleanor, says that the philosophy lessons have rubbed off on her. And like her character, her favored ethical position is moral particularism. She says that now, if she is talking about an ethical issue, she can say things like: "Well, I disagree with that because, you know in moral particularism, cited by [British philosopher] Jonathan Dancy' – like, I actually have a sound argument as to why I believe certain things."

21st Century Dilemmas
The Selfie Generation

Tahani's namedropping and Jason's narcissism are, in part, a reflection of a culture that has become more individualistic and ego-oriented. While moral philosophy is broad enough to encompass the theory that egoism can be either a rational or ethical approach to life, it is hard to believe that it can be morally sound to, for instance, take a selfie in the bathroom at your great-aunt's funeral, as Eleanor did.

In the episode *Rhonda, Diana, Jake, and Trent* we see a museum celebrating awful behavior: replicas of, for instance, the first person to floss their teeth in a public office, the first man to say, "well, actually" to a woman, the first white man to wear dreadlocks, and the first person to call Ultimate Frisbee "ultimate". It seems at times that the real target of the writers of the show isn't so much unethical behavior as boorish superficiality, and a general breakdown in respect and civility. But there is always a crossover between simple boorishness and immoral behavior – flossing in a public office demonstrates an inability to think about other people's point of view, for instance.

Of course, we eventually discover that Tahani's death on Earth was a direct result of her need for attention – her envy of the ridiculous success earned by her pop-star sister causes her to sneak in to her Rock & Roll Hall of Fame induction party, where she is crushed while trying to destroy the giant gold statue of Kamilah.

Jason's case is a more complex one. Some commenters have suggested that his self-interested actions make him a representation of **ethical egoism**. This is the theory that moral agents should do what is in their own self-interest. Jason exposes himself as AcidCat purely to try and ramp up his failing career, he sabotages the girlfriend of a dance crew member to keep the crew together, and he attempts a heist on Chipotle along with his idiotic (but funny) friend Pillboi purely because he wants some money. However, it is probably being too kind to suggest he has an ethical framework at all in his time on Earth. Given that his attempted heist led to him being suffocated in the safe he was hiding in, we should probably instead characterize him either as a moral nihilist or, as Eleanor might say, as simply the dumbest person you are ever likely to meet. (Although when she describes him this way to his face, he is too dumb to realize who she is talking about).

Good vs Bad or Good vs Evil

For all Jason's idiotic behavior, we still come to like him as a human being: we simply don't make all our judgments in life on purely moral grounds, no matter how much Chidi might want us to.

It's also worth mentioning that there are philosophers who reject all the mainstream attempts to define moral philosophy and take wildly different angles. The German philosopher Friedrich Nietzsche often discussed morals (for instance in his book *Beyond Good and Evil*) and generally saw them as being products of the human psyche. He distinguishes "master morality" from "slave morality", arguing that the strong and powerful value pride and power, while slave morality focuses on kindness, empathy, and sympathy – he was scathing about Christian and Kantian moral values, seeing them as the embodiment of slave morality, motivated by *ressentiment,* a seething hatred of the strong and powerful and an attempt to frame morals that would limit their ability to act.

His predecessor Arthur Schopenhauer argued that all human experience comes down to the "will to live" and that morality is about understanding and having compassion for all manifestations of the will to live. Meanwhile numerous more recent philosophers, particularly those of a Marxist persuasion, have seen the field of ethics in terms of political control – the question of whether, for instance, it is right to steal can equally be framed in terms of why private property exists at all and who that institution benefits. Bearing this in mind, Jason, the failed thief, might be comforted by the words of Pierre-Joseph Proudhon: "property is theft".

Fun Fact: **The Soundtrack in Hell**

If you've ever wondered what the soundtrack will be in hell, you need wonder no more. Aside from the Bad Place crew's love for "Who Let The Dogs Out?" and the general aversion to the Red Hot Chili Peppers, Shawn listens to "Right Here Waiting" by Richard Marx when he is in need of something "truly terrible" to inspire him. And when DJ Bad Janet presides over the closing down party for the neighborhood she plays only Puddle of Mudd's "She Hates Me" and Elmo & Patsy's "Grandma Got Run Over by a Reindeer." (And for a grand finale, she plays them both at the same time).

21st Century Dilemmas
Virtue Signaling

When Tahani refers to her planned relief mission to Haiti as an opportunity to be photographed being charitable, this again raises the complex question of whether an action is good if we are doing it for bad reasons. Remember that this is someone who goes out each day to pick orchids for her nightly bath in them. In this case her mission clearly will help people, but if you do it for the cameras or for social media are you doing it for real? The concept of virtue signaling originally came from zoology, where "signaling" is a kind of non-verbal communication. In recent years it has come to be used, mostly in a pejorative sense, to describe self-consciously good acts or statements that are intended to draw attention to the virtuousness of the person acting or speaking.

Of course, the term can also be used in a more dubious way, to undermine the effect of a genuinely good deed or virtuous statement by implying that is has only been done for attention. Basically, you can end up being the kind of dirtbag who would eat a hatful of name slips, lie about who is the nominated driver to be picked from the hat and then imply that your friends' moral outrage demonstrates their lack of "integrity".

As well as wondering whether someone is doing a good

thing for the right reason, we should also take a moment to wonder whether someone making an accusation of virtue signaling might have negative reasons to do so.

Chidi's Challenges

1. Your favourite television show is about to be cancelled. You can save it so the next series gets made, but only if you tell a lie. Do you?

2. What would you add to the soundtrack for your personal Bad Place? How about the Good Place?

3. You make friends with someone, but then find out that they think claustrophobia is fear of Santa Claus and that you should always trust someone wearing a bowtie. What do you do?

The Leap to Faith
Kierkegaard, Nietzsche and Other Dirtbags

The title of this episode in the second season of *The Good Place* is a reference to the work of the Danish philosopher Søren Kierkegaard. We've also seen Chidi staring at the contents of his book *Fear and Trembling* as a kind of self-soothing mechanism when he is stressed out, and heard a couple of lines from his attempt at writing a rap musical about Kierkegaard which rhymes "impeccable" with "teleological suspension of the ethical".

The title of *Fear and Trembling* comes from the bible, from Philippians: Kierkegaard discusses the anxiety that Abraham must have felt after being instructed by God to kill his son Isaac. He argues that rational thought can get stuck in circular loops and prevent you from faith in God, and that the solution to this is a "leap". The phrase used is often translated as "leap of faith" but Chidi pedantically prefers to talk of a "leap into faith" or "leap to faith".

Michael references Kierkegaard in his hilariously unfunny roast of Chidi, suggesting that the four friends need to keep faith and that while he appears to be playing along with Shawn and the Bad Place demons, they need to keep their faith in him. There is a degree to which the entire project of going to the Bad Place to try and escape from their predicament is a leap into faith: after all, Michael has also described their mission as being quintessentially human, as it involves trying something that is almost certainly futile, with a huge amount of unwarranted confidence that is likely to lead to failure. On the journey, Chidi is forced to make a similarly awful leap – every Kantian bone in his body is telling him not to lie: as a professor of moral philosophy he has already explained numerous times that he doesn't like lying and won't advise someone else to do so. No matter how many times Eleanor demonstrates how white lies can be useful, he remains reluctant to follow her lead.

Fun Fact: **The Real Professors of Moral Philosophy**

One reason why the philosophical content of *The Good Place* is so accurate is that Michael Schur consulted regularly with academics who were specialists in ethics – in particular Pamela Hieronymi, a professor of philosophy at the University of California in Los Angeles, and Todd May, a professor of philosophy at Clemson University in South Carolina, have acted as consultants, talking Schur through the subjects that inform the storylines of the show, and the topics that Chidi is teaching.

Keeping Secrets

The subject of keeping secrets is a surprisingly important part of romantic relationships. We mostly believe that there are some situations in which keeping a secret is relatively harmless. While Eleanor is fretting about whether she should tell Chidi she has seen a video of the two of them in bed together and clearly in love, she asks for his advice: he tells her that it is acceptable to keep secrets so long as it doesn't harm anyone and the telling of the secret isn't going to cause harm.

She is initially satisfied with this surprisingly flexible answer, as it gives her the lazy, easy option of not telling him. However, what is love, if it is not about sharing everything with your soulmate? The idea of honesty is an integral part of how two people can come together and make up a single unit. We share our true selves with the person we love.

But even when we are deeply in love with someone, we may choose not to tell them every uncomfortable little truth – for instance whether you find that actor or actress attractive or not. White lies on subjects like this can sometimes feel better than the whole, unvarnished truth.

Of course, in the end Eleanor feels that it is not her right to decide whether her secret will cause harm, and fesses up about the video. Where that will eventually lead, we don't yet know, but it is clear that the mere possibility of romance between the two is central to the ongoing narrative of the show.

Fun Fact: **Ted's Secret**

When Ted Danson was cast, he had to keep the secret that Michael turns out not to be what he seems: when he told people the fake plot of his new show, they seemed bored so he kept blurting out the truth and giving away the twist that ends the first season. He has said "I was wracked with guilt, but luckily the people I told, I called them and said, 'Please, dear God, [don't tell anyone],' but all of my friends are so self-obsessed that they'd probably forgotten already what I had told them."

Eternal Recurrence

Without revealing every detail of the plot, we realize early in the second season of *The Good Place* that the neighborhood Eleanor lives in can be endlessly "rebooted", so no matter how many times Eleanor comes to the same realization about their fate, she can be taken back to live a slightly different version of her predicament. When Chidi talks to her about the problem, he describes it as being like a twisted alternative version of Nietzsche's

eternal recurrence – they have the basic experience of karma but aren't given the chance to learn from their repetitive experiences. (Eleanor dismisses his insight with the comment that even when Chidi has a nightmare, it's boring).

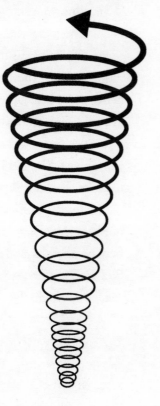

The idea that the universe is cyclical is an ancient one – it can be found in the writings of early Hindu scholars and in the work of the pre-Socratic Greek philosophers, for instance. For Nietzsche, eternal recurrence is a kind of thought experiment which forces you to put the utmost weight on every moral decision. He writes: "What, if some day or night a demon were to steal after you into your loneliest loneliness and say to you: 'This life as you now live it and have lived it, you will have to live once more and innumerable times more; and there will be nothing new in it, but every pain and every joy and every thought and sigh and everything unutterably small or great in your life will have to return to you, all in the same succession and sequence – even this spider and this moonlight between the trees, and even this moment and I myself.'"

Imagine you are in a video game, and you will have to keep reliving the same sequence over and over. His suggestion is that your reaction to this idea is a test of your moral courage and how well you are living your life: the better the life, the less distressing this idea would be. And, as a consequence, the way to live a good life is to make every moral decision with that heavy weight hanging over it: ask yourself, what would I do right now if I knew I would have to make this same decision over and over forever?

Of course, for Eleanor and Chidi, this is not an option: not being in control of the cycle means that, while there may be one reboot out there where they fall in love and find true happiness, they are unable to keep to that "best version of themselves" and make it stick.

Fun Fact

While the Bad Place has some subtle, loopy ways of punishing its residents, we are also given a few glimpses of old-school hell and brimstone. In the first episode Janet plays a brief but terrifying audio clip of people screaming as they are tortured there. And the almighty judge later refers to some of the old-fashioned tools at the disposal of demons in the Bad Place including "the old penis-flattener" and "butthole spiders", to which he adds: "They're enormous".

Chidi's Challenges

Test your ethical development, with a few more questions . . .

1. You run into Ted Danson, who is working behind the bar in your local drinking hole. He offers to tell you what happens at the end of the next series of *The Good Place*. What do you do?

2. Your father takes you into the mountains, ties you up and tells you that he has heard the voice of God telling him to kill you as a sacrifice. At the last minute he hears an angel telling him not to go through with it. What do you do next?

3. Imagine that you will have to live this week over and over for all of eternity. Do you think you're making the best possible use of your time?

Everything is Bonzer!
Medium People and Their Consciences

One question which moral philosophy professors get exercised about is crime and the punishment – Nietzsche doubted that punishment serves any purpose, writing that it "is supposed to have the value of arousing the *feeling of guilt* in the guilty party", but that it mostly failed to achieve this: "On the whole, punishment makes men harder and colder, it concentrates, it sharpens the feeling of alienation; it strengthens the power to resist." It can also be argued that the message sent by punishing a criminal isn't that he has done something innately wrong, but that he has got himself on the wrong team – after all, why are the other team allowed to do "bad things" to him?

A similar problem arises when we consider the idea of heaven and hell. If good acts are inspired by a desire to go to heaven and a fear of hell, is this not a classic problem of moral desert, in which we expect to be rewarded for our virtue? And why would we learn how to be good by fearing the tortures of the Bad Place – for instance the flying piranhas and lava monsters, hotdog insertions, being made to organize baby showers for people, or to eat egg salad from a vending machine in Azerbaijan?

Furthermore, how can a system even be moral if someone like the Good Eleanor Shellstrop (whose place "Fake Eleanor" has taken) can be subjected to such heinous tortures because of a mere administrative cock-up.

The Good Place gives us a partial answer to this: Eleanor doesn't become good purely from the ethics lessons, or because of moral desert. She learns to listen to her conscience. After she picks up the trash, Chidi tells Eleanor that it is positive she is feeling remorse about doing something bad (which isn't as good as doing the right thing, but at least it is a start). But she has always had some level of remorse and conscience. In the past, when she made dirtbag decisions like stealing olives in the store, then spitting the pits on the floor, watching an old man slip over and fall having stepped on her pits and then going back for a second helping while the staff are distracted, there was a small voice in the back of her head telling her this wasn't the right thing to do. It was partly because of the discomfort that the voice caused that she felt the need to drag other people down to her level.

When she learns to behave better, she is relieved by the absence of that voice. Her conscience is no longer nagging at her because she is making the right decisions, at least for a while. And when she slips from the path of virtue, she happily has Michael to give her a nudge in the right direction (which just happens to be Australia).

Chidi may be a good influence on Eleanor and he may be able to explain all the rational reasons why certain actions are good or bad. But ultimately the only person she truly needs to listen to is that voice in her head, her own conscience. As Lao Tzu once wrote: "knowing others is wisdom but knowing the self is enlightenment."

Trevor's Greatest Moments

While Eleanor is presented as being somewhere between a dirtbag and a medium person, we are given at least one example of pure evil in the form of Trevor. It's Trevor who tries to cajole Eleanor into going to the Bad Place on the basis that she will be happier there even though he'll be torturing her, because she won't have to try and pretend to be good anymore.

Trevor also cuts his toenails at the dinner table and sends wine back just to show the waiter he is superior, has 100 Hawaiian pizzas delivered to Michael's office, and lies about having slept with Eleanor (asking who people will believe, him or "a woman"). And when he is in charge of the train to the Bad Place, he points out that the food service would consist only of clam chowder at room temperature, if it were open, which it isn't. And, most damning of all, he is a fan of *The Bachelor*. The only crimes he doesn't confess to are having paid money to watch the Red Hot Chili Peppers perform live music, and using the office microwave to cook fish, but we know deep down he probably does those too.

The Medium Place

In the penultimate episode of the first season of *The Good Place,* we are introduced to Mindy St Claire. She was a corporate lawyer who mainly cared about sex, money and cocaine when she was alive. However, one night she had a vision of a foundation that would transform global agriculture, help kids everywhere, and generally make the world a much better place. She unfortunately fell onto some rail tracks and died before putting her plan into action, but her sister took over and made it happen.

A dispute between the Good Place and the Bad Place over whether she deserves the credit for the wonderful consequences of her coked-up idea has led to her being the sole resident of the Medium Place. This seems like a pretty mediocre place to live, as the Bad Place have messed with it just enough to sabotage most fun that could be had there – Mindy has a supply of beer, but no fridge so she has to drink it warm, and her entertainment for eternity consists of a tiny TV, a VHS tape of *Cannonball Run II* and a single *People* magazine featuring Pierce Brosnan.

Eleanor is frequently drawn to the idea of running away to the Medium Place. She clearly doesn't belong in the Good Place, but the Bad Place seems too harsh a punishment for someone like her, who sucked but "in a fun, chill way". And she has shown she can do good things. When Michael gives her the basic good and bad litmus test we find that she hasn't killed anyone or committed arson, she hasn't taken off her shoes and socks on a commercial flight, and she has never paid money to see the Red Hot Chili Peppers. And Eleanor is capable of kindness – her cousin is a bit of a mess, so she takes her daughter Julie to the mall for a break sometimes. Admittedly she proceeds to feed her Arizona trash food like Churro Dogs (a hot dog between two churros tied together with a Slim Jim) but it shows her heart can sometimes be in the right place.

In spite of her many failings, it doesn't seem fair for someone like her to be completely forked by being eternally damned. Before she even knows about Mindy, she has commented that there should be a Medium Place (somewhere like Cincinnati) for people like her.

This is one of the key themes of *The Good Place*. Most of us will recognize a bit of ourselves in the flawed characters we are watching – none of them are perfect, they have upset other people and lost points for bad choices. But there is a kind of redemption in the friendship they show each other.

We're probably mostly medium people like them; we don't deserve harps and clouds, but nor do we deserve hot spike pits, lava bees or lightning that tears our flesh off for eternity. What ethics can do for us is to focus our attention on the ways we can be slightly better versions of ourselves – it won't turn sinners into saints, but it might at least make us medium-good, rather than medium-bad.

Conclusion
Being Good

The study of moral philosophy can be frustrating as there are lots of difficult questions and no easy answers. That's why moral philosophy professors are so unpopular. But *The Good Place* shines a light on some of the most interesting themes of ethics and challenges us to think about what it truly means to be good. At a key point in the series Eleanor tells Chidi how grateful she is to him for his selfless help: she says it's like she found herself in a dark cave, and he was her flashlight. This is a reference to Plato's Allegory of the Cave – he compares humans to people in a cave who are seeing shadows on the wall – true forms like Good, Virtue and Truth are outside the cave, and we can only perceive them through their shadows.

This has an obvious parallel to the plight of Eleanor, Chidi, Tahani and Jason in the neighborhood – there is a greater truth out there which they can only discover through hints and clues. But it is also a nice analogy for the role of ethical theory in our lives – it can't tell us the precise truth about what is "good" or "virtuous" – but it can nonetheless help us to live better and to be in a good place in our own lives.

The Good Place is a rare thing – a genuinely funny comedy that provokes us to ponder some of the deepest questions of our existence: can we become a better person? Is there an afterlife? Do we have souls or soulmates? Which, if any, religion can tell us more than about 5% of the truth? Where will we go after we die, and will it be like the heaven or hell we can read about in holy books? And more importantly, will they be serving frozen yogurt or clam chowder?

Everything will be fine.

Glossary

Altruism: the idea that you should act in the interests of other people.

Categorical imperative: Immanuel Kant's term for a kind of moral rule that you should follow in any conceivable circumstance, as you couldn't reasonably wish the opposite to be a universal moral rule.

Cognitivist error theory: the idea that ethical statements do make sense, but are universally false.

Cognitivist realism: the idea that ethical statements make sense and can be either true or false.

Consequentialist: the blanket term for ethical systems that are based on consequences and outcomes of actions.

Contractarianism: an ethical theory, promoted for instance by Thomas Scanlon, in which the justification for co-operating with a central state or authority is based in the self-interest of everyone. A type of social contract theory.

Contractualism: a type of social contract theory which emphasizes how reasonable or justifiable rules are to other people – the veil of ignorance promoted by John Rawls is an example.

Deontology: the blanket term for ethical systems that attempt to develop definite rules that we should always follow: examples include the categorical imperative, divine command, intuitionism and social contract theory.

Divine command: the idea that ethical rules are handed down from a God or higher being.

Double effect, doctrine of: the idea that if our action has a morally bad side-effect, it's not necessarily wrong, providing the bad side-effect wasn't intended, even if it was foreseeable.

Eternal recurrence: the idea (derived from Friedrich Nietzsche) that we should act as though we know we will have to make the same decision an infinite number of times as we are living in an eternal loop.

Ethical egoism: the idea that ethics should be based in acting in the self-interest.

Eudemonism: the ancient Greek view that it is ethical to act in the manner that will maximize happiness.

Evolutionary ethics: the idea that ethical rules and statements are based in evolutionary, biological imperatives.

Existentialism: the philosophical idea that existence is meaningless, which leads to the ethical idea that we must take responsibility for our own actions rather than looking to moral rules or higher beings.

Golden rule: Jesus's basic moral rules that we should do unto others as we would have them do to us.

Ideal observer: in subjectivist ethics, moral rules are often formed by asking the question "what would an imaginary impartial observer of this situation believe is the right thing to do?".

Intellectual virtue: the kind of virtue that, according to Aristotle, can be taught and learned throughout life.

Intuitionism: the idea that we have a simple, direct sense of what good is and can recognize it when we encounter it.

Leap to faith: Søren Kierkegaard's idea that rational thought can trap us in circular thinking and that we need to make the leap to believing in God.

Meta-ethics: the study of what sort of thing an ethical statement is.

Moral desert: the idea that we should do the right thing for its own sake, without doing it either because we are seeking a reward or trying to avoid punishment.

Moral particularism: the view that there are no moral principles and that moral judgment can be found only as one decides particular cases, either real or imagined.

Moral perfectionism: the idea, espoused by Jonathan Dancy, that there are no moral rules that can help us in every situation, and that nothing is good or bad regardless of context.

Moral virtue: according to Aristotle, the basic moral character we are born with or develop as children which consequently can't be learned as an adult.

Natural rights: the idea (espoused by John Locke among others) that humans are born with certain inalienable rights which we can define and which should be the basis of moral and legal rules.

Non-cognitivism: the idea that when we make an ethical statement it is not really about ethics but expresses our preferences (prescriptivism), emotions (emotivism) or attitudes (quasi-realism).

Normative ethics: the attempt to create systems which define what kind of things are morally correct.

Practical ethics: the study of how to behave morally in particular situations in life.

Rationalism: the idea that we make rational assessments of our situation and choose how to act morally on that basis.

Situational ethics: the blanket term for ethical theories that reject the idea of absolute rules that will work in all situations.

Slippery slope: the idea that one small immoral act might lead, through an inevitable chain of consequences, to a much greater wrong.

Social contract theory: any theory which proposes that moral rules arise out of negotiation or unwritten agreements between members of a society.

Social conventions: some deontological theories suggest that ethical rules are simply social conventions: an example of this kind of thinking is social contract theory.

Social intuitionism: the psychological theory that, as opposed to rationalist thought, our moral choices arise from our emotions and intuitions, rather than from rational judgment.

Subjectivism: the idea that all moral judgments are subjective and dependent on situation, culture or time.

Thought experiment: a story about a situation which is designed to test our emotional responses. Examples include the trolley problem, which is designed to test our intuitions on how to choose when we have to decide who should live or die, and the violinist, which is designed to explore moral attitudes to abortion.

Utilitarianism: the consequentialist idea that we should calculate the happiness and pain that will be caused by a proposed action and act so as to maximize happiness. Classical utilitarianism focuses on individual happiness, while welfare utilitarianism identifies happiness with economic well-being.

Veil of ignorance: in the contractualist theory espoused by John Rawls, we are asked to imagine all the members of a society drawing up the rules from behind a veil of ignorance which prevents them from knowing what role they will be allotted within that society.

Virtue ethics: the blanket term for any ethical theory which focuses on individual character and moral virtue rather than on rules or consequences.

Virtue signaling: performing a good act in the hope that it will be noticed and will bring you praise.

Further Reading

Season 1
Episode 1: Everything Is Fine
The Fundamentals of Ethics, Russ Shafer-Landau: This isn't referenced in the series, but is a good overview of ethics which gives the reader a good grounding in the general topics covered.

Episode 2: Flying
Metaphysics of Morals, Immanuel Kant: Chidi refers to this title in order to explain the concept of selflessness to Eleanor.

Episode 3: Tahani Al-Jamil
The Nicomachean Ethics, Aristotle: This is one of the first works referenced in Chidi's attempts to teach Eleanor about ethics.

Episode 4: Jason Mendoza
A Treatise on Human Nature, David Hume: Eleanor expresses bemusement after attempting to read this book twice.

Episode 5: Category 55 Emergency Doomsday Crisis
Utilitarianism, John Stuart Mill: Eleanor is initially impressed by the simplicity of utilitarianism, although Chidi explains that it does have some pitfalls.

Episode 6: What We Owe to Each Other
What We Owe to Each Other, Thomas Scanlon: When Chidi has to explain social contract theory on the spot to Eleanor, he uses the example of this title. (We will also see Eleanor watching part of his three-hour Internet lecture on the title.)

Episode 7: The Eternal Shriek
The Prince, Machiavelli: This is a book that is profoundly amoral in its approach, as Chidi explains when he refutes Eleanor's suggestion that the end (saving Michael) might justify the means (killing Janet).

Episode 8: Most Improved Player
On a Supposed Right to Lie from Philanthropic Concerns, Immanuel Kant: This 1799 work elaborates on the view

of Kant (whom Eleanor casually cites, impressing Chidi) that lying (as she wants him to do for her) is always wrong.

Episode 9: . . . Someone Like Me as a Member

Lying: Moral Choice in Public and Private Life, Sissela Bok: Not directly referenced in the series, this is one of the best books ever written on the ethics of lying (as Eleanor asks Chidi to do for her).

Episode 10: Chidi's Choice

The Symposium, Plato: Chidi's indecision about his soulmate has interesting parallels in this dialectical work.

Episode 11: What's My Motivation

An Introduction to the Principles of Morals and Legislation, Jeremy Bentham: Eleanor laboriously attempts to build up her points total, as a utilitarian ethicist such as Bentham (John Stuart Mill's predecessor) might have suggested.

Episode 12: Mindy St Claire

After Virtue: A Study in Moral Theory, Alasdair MacIntyre: MacIntyre's exploration of virtue ethics comes to mind as we meet Mindy St Claire, a person of mostly bad character who happened to do one outstandingly good thing.

Episode 13: Michael's Gambit

The Republic, Plato: As Eleanor discovers the truth about the Good Place, you might want to ponder the question of what kind of world you would create if you were in the role of architect or "philosopher king" as imagined by Socrates in this book.

Season 2

Episodes 14-15: Everything Is Great! (Parts 1 and 2)

Theodicy, Gottfried Wilhelm Leibniz: Leibniz famously argued that the world we live in the best of all possible worlds, in other words the best world God could have created. Eleanor, Chidi and friends might dispute that by this stage of the story.

Episode 16: Dance Dance Resolution

The Gay Science, Friedrich Nietzsche: The concept of eternal recurrence is discussed in this title, which also happens to be one of Nietzsche's most accessible works. (He is a writer who is often funny and provocative, in spite of his dour, negative reputation.)

Episode 17: Team Cockroach

The Infinite Tortoise, Joel Levy: Michael asks the humans to co-operate with him – the prisoners, dilemma is a thought experiment about when it is right to co-operate with others, one of many such dilemmas discussed in this brief guide.

Episode 18: Existential Crisis
The Age of Reason, Jean-Paul Sartre: Many existentialist books are dense and hard to read – Sartre's fictional trilogy *The Roads to Freedom*, of which this is the first title, explores the concept of freedom through episodes from the life of philosophy teacher Mathieu, and is a much more enjoyable read than (for instance) *Being and Nothingness*.

Episode 19: The Trolley Problem
The Problem of Abortion and the Doctrine of the Double Effect, Philippa Foot: The original formulation of this problem was given in this essay (although it has also been discussed by many later writers).

Episode 20: Janet and Michael
An Essay Concerning Human Understanding, John Locke: Janet struggles to maintain "object permanence". This connects to the Ship of Theseus, one of many topics discussed in Locke's classic – the ship, which is constantly rebuilt at sea, ends up being made of completely different material – the comparison is with human physical and mental identity.

Episode 21: Derek

A Theory of Justice, John Rawls: one of Chidi's favourite philosophers, Rawls discusses the moral foundations of decisions such as "should we kill Derek?" and grounds this in his version of social contract theory.

Episode 22: Leap to Faith

Fear and Trembling, Søren Kierkegaard: This is the source of the idea of the "leap into faith" and a fascinating, if difficult read.

Episode 23: Best Self

Practical Ethics, Peter Singer: The humans wrestle with the idea of being their best self (and, in particular, Chidi frets about his use of almond milk): Peter Singer's excellent work explores many such everyday dilemmas such as "is it OK to buy luxuries that people in the third world are denied?" or "is it OK to have a higher than average carbon footprint?"

Episode 24: Rhonda, Diana, Jake, and Trent

Ethics Without Principles, Jonathan Dancy: As Eleanor decides she is a moral particularist, this is one of several excellent works by Dancy, the main proponent of this system of ethical thought.

Episode 25: The Burrito

The Object of Morality, G. J. Warnock: As the friends attempt to avoid condemnation to the Bad Place, we are once again asked 'what is a good person?' Warnock's book is a fascinating exploration of what morality is actually for, and whether we need it in our lives to make the world a less intolerable place.

Episode 26: Somewhere Else

Anarchy, State and Utopia, Robert Nozick: John Rawls rejected the idea that anyone ever deserves credit or reward for a moral act (the concept of moral desert as referenced by the judge in this episode): Nozick famously took issue with Rawls on this and gives a justification of moral desert in this book.

Season 3 and beyond

When you get to the Good Place, check your bookshelf for an updated version of this book which will cover every episode ever (although it might be 1,000 pages long, full of spoilers and as unreadable as Chidi's epic work on ethics – that's why everyone hates moral philosophy writers).

Acknowledgments

Many thanks to my wife and daughter for putting up with my own ethical shortcomings. I also owe belated gratitude to those teachers at college who helped me wrestle with the history of ethics in the first place, including (but not limited to) Tom Baldwin, David Hugh Mellor, Michael Tanner, Jimmy Altham, and (briefly but memorably) Jonathan Lear.